We Believe & Celebrate

Parish Director's Guide

First PENANCE ✠ First COMMUNION
SADLIER SACRAMENT PROGRAM

Sadlier
A Division of William H. Sadlier, Inc.

Sadlier's *We Believe & Celebrate* program was developed by the community of faith through representatives with expertise in liturgy, theology, Scripture, catechesis, and children's faith development. This program leads to a deeper experience of Jesus in the community and springs from the wisdom of this community.

We Believe & Celebrate Program
Catechetical and Liturgical Consultants
Dr. Gerard F. Baumbach
Director, Center for Catechetical Initiatives
Concurrent Professor of Theology
University of Notre Dame

Sr. Janet Baxendale, SC
Adjunct Professor of Liturgy
St. Joseph Seminary, Dunwoodie, NY

Carole M. Eipers, D.Min.
Vice President
Executive Director of Catechetics
William H. Sadlier, Inc.

Rev. Ronald J. Lewinski, S.T.L
St. Mary of the Annunciation
Mundelein, IL

Rev. Msgr. James P. Moroney
Executive Director of the USCCB
Secretariat for the Liturgy

Curriculum and Child Development Consultants
Patricia Andrews
Director of Religious Education
Our Lady of Lourdes
Slidell, LA

William Bishoff
Director of Catechetical Ministries
Mission San Luis Rey Parish
Oceanside, CA

Diana Carpenter
Director of Faith Formation
St. Elizabeth Ann Seton Parish
San Antonio, TX

Inculturation Consultants
Dulce M. Jimenez-Abreu
Director of Spanish Programs
William H. Sadlier, Inc.

Vilma Angulo
Director of Religious Education
All Saints Catholic Church
Sunrise, FL

Media/Technology Consultant
Sister Jane Keegan, RDC
Senior Internet Editor
William H. Sadlier, Inc.

Theological Consultants
Most Reverend Edward K. Braxton,
    Ph.D, S.T.D.
Official Theological Consultant
Bishop of Belleville

Monsignor John Arnold, Vicar General
Archdiocese of Westminister

Sadlier Consulting Team
Roy Arroyo
Michaela Burke
Judith Devine

Ken Doran
William M. Ippolito
Saundra Kennedy, Ed.D.
Kathleen Krane
Suzan Larroquette

Parish Director's Guide
Writing/Development Team
Rosemary K. Calicchio
Vice President of Publications

Melissa Gibbons
Product Director

Kathleen Hendricks
Contributing Writer

Christopher Weber
Contributing Writer

Blake Bergen
Editorial Director

Allie Connors
Editor

Electronic Media
Michael Ferejohn
Director

Toby Carson

Erik Bowie

Publishing Operations Team
Deborah J. Jones
Vice President of Publishing Operations

Vince Gallo
Creative Director

Francesca O'Malley
Associate Art Director

Jim Saylor
Photography Manager

Jovito Pagkalinawan
Electronic Prepress Manager

Design Staff
Kevin Butler
Sasha Khorovsky

Production Staff
Douglas Labidee
Gavin Smith

Photo Credits
Jane Bernard: 41, 80. Karen Callaway: 63. Crosiers/Gene Plaisted, OSC: 55 *top*, 75 *top*. Neal Farris: 15, 25, 27, 69–71, 78, 79 *center right*, 8, 83. Getty Images/Digital Vision: 8 *top*. Ken Karp: 5 *top left*, 79 *bottom center*. Masterfile/Ariel Skelley: 22. Photodisc Red: 8 *bottom*. Veer: 62. Superstock/Kwame Zikomo: 9. Bill Wittman: 55 *bottom center*.

Illustrator Credits
Teresa Berassi: 73 *top*. Mary Bono: 34, 67. Mircea Catusanu: 46. Dean MacAdam: 6, 33, 82. Diane Magnuson: 57, 68. Judith Moffatt:
45, 48, 66 *bottom right*. Jackie Snider: 6, 66 *top left*, 77. W.B. Johnston: 3, 13, 20, 21, 23, 27, 31, 39, 49, 51, 56, 64, 73 *bottom*, 75, 76 *right*, 78 *top*, 84.

Acknowledgments
Scripture excerpts are taken from the *New American Bible with Revised New Testament and Psalms*. Copyright © 1991, 1986, 1970, Confraternity of Christian Doctrine, Inc. Washington, D.C. Used with permission. All rights reserved. No portion of the *New American Bible* may be reprinted without permission in writing from the copyright holder.

Excerpts from the *National Directory for Catechesis* © 2005, United States Conference of Catholic Bishops, Washington, D.C. All rights reserved. No part of this work may be reproduced or transmitted in any form without the permission in writing from the copyright holder.

Excerpts from the English translation of *Rite of Penance* © 1974, International Committee on English in the Liturgy, Inc. (ICEL); excerpts from the English translation of *The Roman Missal* © 1973, ICEL; excerpts from the English translation of *Rite of Confirmation* (2nd Edition) © 1975, ICEL. All rights reserved.

Excerpts from *Catholic Household Blessings and Prayers* Copyright © 1988, United States Catholic Conference, Inc. Washington, D.C. All rights reserved.

From *Extending the Table: A World Community Cookbook* by Joetta Handrich Schlabach. © 1991 by Herald Press, Pennsylvania.

From *The Secrets of Jesuit Soupmaking: A Year of Our Soups* by Rick Curry. © 2002 by Penguin Books, New York.

"A Circle of Love," © 1991, Felicia Sandler. Published by OCP Publications, 5536 NE Hassalo, Portland, OR 97213. All rights reserved. "Open Our Hearts," © 1989, Christopher Walker. Published by OCP Publications, 5536 NE Hassalo, Portland, OR 97213. All rights reserved. "Take the Word of God with You," text © 1991, James Harrison. Music © 1991, Christopher Walker. Text and music published by OCP Publications, 5536 NE Hassalo, Portland, OR 97213. All rights reserved. "We Remember You," © 1999, Bernadette Farrell. Published by OCP Publications, 5536 NE Hassalo, Portland, OR 97213. All rights reserved. "Jesus, You Are Bread for Us," © 1988, Christopher Walker. Published by OCP Publications, 5536 NE Hassalo, Portland, OR 97213. All rights reserved.

William H. Sadlier, Inc.
9 Pine Street
New York, NY 10005-1002

ISBN: 0-8215-5719-X
123456789/10 9 08 07 06

This advanced copy has been printed prior to final publication and pending ecclesiastical approval.

Table of Contents

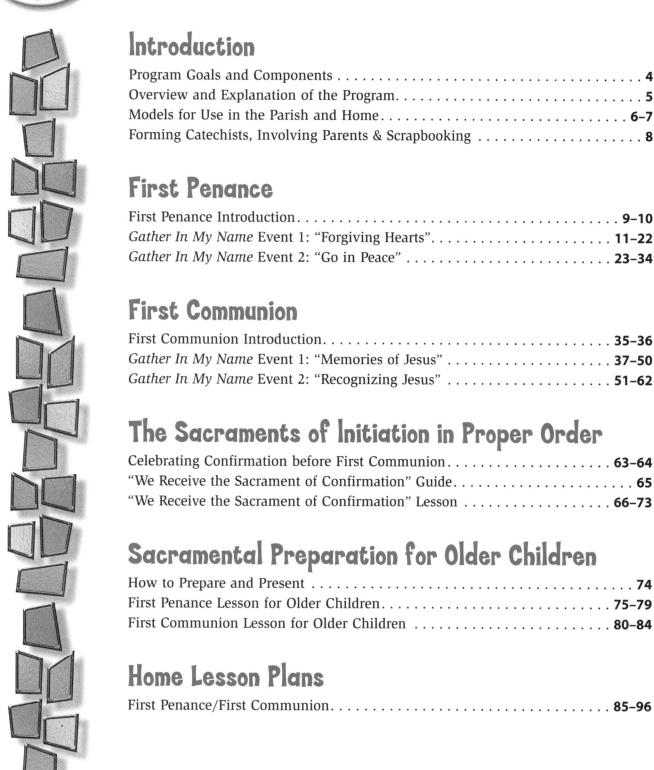

Introduction

First Penance

First Communion

The Sacraments of Initiation in Proper Order

Sacramental Preparation for Older Children

Home Lesson Plans

For your faith journey:

One of the first things I ever learned about Jesus was . . .

I first recognized Jesus in the Eucharist . . .

I first experienced God's forgiveness in the Sacrament of Penance . . .

Dear Parish Director:

You play a critical role in the parish. You not only lead children to their celebration of First Penance and First Communion, you help entire households recognize the meaning of these sacraments in their lives. To help you to assist families in the immediate preparation of their children for First Communion and First Penance, Sadlier's *We Believe & Celebrate First Penance* and *First Communion* follows three main goals:

Goal 1: To provide age-appropriate catechesis on the celebration and reception of the sacraments to children

Goal 2: To facilitate the role of parents in the sacramental preparation of their children

Goal 3: To provide catechesis that "is intended for all members of the Christian community, takes place within the community, and involves the whole community of faith" (*NDC*, 35B).

The following components engage children and their parents in the learning process:

- *We Believe & Celebrate First Penance* and *First Communion* keepsake books (student texts) help children learn about each sacrament and include scrapbooking options to create treasured family memories to last for a lifetime.

- *We Believe & Celebrate First Penance* and *First Communion Guides* offer easy-to-follow lesson plans for the catechist, scrapbooking helps, and flexible options for family use.

- *We Believe & Celebrate First Penance* and *First Communion Home Lesson Plans* are practical and family-friendly tools to help parents prepare their children to celebrate the sacraments.

- The *We Believe & Celebrate First Penance/First Communion Music CD* enhances lessons and provides songs for prayer celebrations.

- *We Believe & Celebrate First Penance* Certificates (pad of 24)

- *We Believe & Celebrate First Communion* Certificates (pad of 24)

- *First Penance* Heart Medallions (pack of 10)

- *First Communion* Cross Medallions (pack of 10)

- *With Jesus Always* is a colorful keepsake that helps children participate fully in the Mass and the Sacrament of Penance and Reconciliation.

This Parish Director's Guide brings all of the *We Believe & Celebrate* resources together to promote family learning. Then, it goes one step further, helping you implement Goal 3, the catechesis of the entire parish community. The centerpiece of this implementation is the intergenerational *Gather In My Name* (*GIMN*) events. Two events are provided in this Parish Director's Guide for each sacrament. Parishioners from the wider community can join First Penance and First Communion families at these fun, catechetically sound, and inspiring sessions. As parents, children, and parishioners eat, pray, share faith, and learn together, young and old parishioners alike gain new insights into the sacraments as gifts for a lifetime of faith.

As you implement this program, remember:

- It is your journey of faith, too. Allow the memories, stories of faith, teaching, and questions of others deepen your own faith in the sacraments. "For your faith journey" statements throughout this guide contain key themes of the *Gather In My Name* events. Reflect upon them. Complete the statements. Consider starting your own scrapbook to capture your memories of leading and sharing in this preparation process.

- The entire community makes this journey. The Church is One Body in Christ (I Corinthians 12:12–13), and no member acts in isolation. As children are brought to the Sacraments of Penance and Eucharist, Christ not only fills them with grace, but also blesses and enriches the entire Church. Let this principle guide your planning.

Don't forget our web site!
www.webelieveandcelebrate.com contains color versions of important pages and handouts in this guide, plus many other supplemental resources. Look for this icon throughout the Guide for web-based resources.

ONLINE COMPONENTS
Visit www.webelieveandcelebrate.com

Explanation of the Program

Overview

We Believe & Celebrate provides immediate preparation for a child's first reception of the Sacraments of Penance and Eucharist. This program prepares children in the context of their families and their parish community and leads to the celebration of the sacraments. This Parish Director's Guide will help you bring all of the *We Believe & Celebrate* components together.

- **Parent Letters** highlight the parent and guardian's responsibility in leading the entire household to the sacraments.

- **Getting Started** sections offer valuable tips for scheduling, program design, and liturgical celebrations.

- There is an additional **Confirmation lesson** for parishes celebrating the Proper Order of the Sacraments of Initiation.

- There are also **lessons for older children** who will receive First Penance and First Communion.

- **www.webelieveandcelebrate.com** provides additional parish and family resources for a comprehensive and organized program.

- The *Gather In My Name* events in this guide involve the entire parish community in celebrating First Penance and First Communion with the children and their families.

Get the Whole Community Involved!

This guide and and our web site provide everything you need to offer two *Gather In My Name* events for each sacrament. Developed as an alternative to the conventional parent meeting, these intergenerational sessions will engage your entire parish community in the preparation process. *Gather In My Name* events include:

- an optional meal with recipes to match the event's theme

- an ice-breaker to introduce each session

- opening and closing prayer celebrations

- activities for First Penance and First Communion candidates, their families, and other participants

- small group learning experiences with breakout options by age

- a parish keepsake scrapbooking activity in which participants add pages to a scrapbook for the parish.

Parish directors can use *Gather In My Name* events with groups of any size or scope. While events have been designed to include the entire parish community, parishes wishing to follow a parent meeting format can plan these events exclusively for the households of children receiving these sacraments for the first time. Event outlines will work for a tiny gathering of two or three families or for a crowded parish hall with more than five hundred people. The only limit to the number of participants is the size of the room and the imagination of the director!

You may have to prioritize attendance based upon available space or other resources. However, even if you offer the *Gather In My Name* events just for families of children preparing to celebrate the sacraments, we strongly recommend that you consider inviting select representatives from the greater community. These might include:

- members of the Pastoral Council or religious education board

- key liturgical ministers

- parishioners who by their lived example demonstrate a love for the Sacraments of Penance and Eucharist.

These representatives will play an important role in encouraging the entire parish to join with the children and their families in celebration. Certain *Gather In My Name* events suggest representatives from specific groups to highlight the particular theme of the event.

ONLINE COMPONENTS
Visit www.webelieveandcelebrate.com

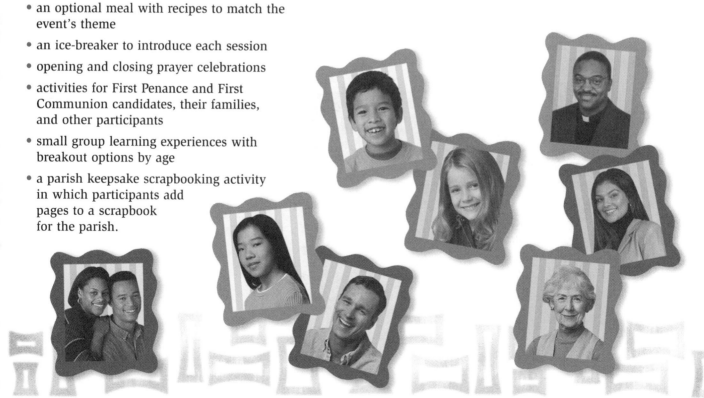

5

Models for Using *We Believe & Celebrate*

You can adapt *We Believe & Celebrate* to multiple models of sacramental preparation. Some parishes train catechists to teach children at the parish. Others encourage parents and guardians to teach their children at home. Still others use a combination of parish-based and home-based catechesis. Select the option that works best for your parish and tailor the *We Believe & Celebrate* components accordingly. Here are three strategies you can use for scheduling the components:

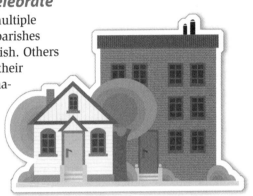

Model 1: Parish-Based Catechesis

Parish-based Components	Home-based Components
Send Parent Letter 1: *Welcome*	
Gather In My Name Event 1 Distribution of keepsake books, heart or cross medallions, and parent information	
Catechists teach sessions 1 to 4 in **keepsake books** using the **First Penance** or **First Communion Guide**	Parents and guardians review chapters with children, assist children in developing scrapbook pages, and work on the "Family Time" pages from the **First Penance** or **First Communion Guide**
Send Parent Letter 2: *Readiness*	
Gather In My Name Event 2	
Catechists teach sessions 5 and 6 in **keepsake books** using the **First Penance** or **First Communion Guide**	Parents and guardians review chapters, assist with scrapbook pages, discern readiness of their children to receive sacrament, and keep working on the "Family Time" pages from the **First Penance** or **First Communion Guide**
Option: Individual Readiness Meetings between the pastor or his delegate and each child and parent	
Rehearsal and celebration of First Penance or First Communion	

Model 2: Parish and Home-Based Catechesis

Parish-based Components	Home-based Components
Send Parent Letter 1: *Welcome*	
Gather In My Name Event 1 Distribution of keepsake books, heart or cross medallions, and parent information	
Catechists teach Sessions 1 and 2 from **keepsake books** in the parish, using **First Penance** or **First Communion Guide**, with parents in attendance	Parents and guardians teach Sessions 3 to 4 from **keepsake books**, assist children in developing scrapbook pages, and work on the "Family Time" pages from the **First Penance** or **First Communion Guide**
Send Parent Letter 2: *Readiness*	
Gather In My Name Event 2	
Catechists teach Session 5 from **keepsake books** in the parish, using **First Penance** or **First Communion Guide**, with parents in attendance	Parents and guardians teach session 6, review chapters, assist with scrapbook pages, work on the "Family Time" pages from the **First Penance** or **First Communion Guide**, and discern readiness of their children to receive sacrament
Option: Individual Readiness Meetings between the pastor or his delegate and each child and parent	
Rehearsal and celebration of First Penance or First Communion	

Model 3: Home-Based Catechesis

Parish-based Components	Home-based Components
Send Parent Letter 1: *Welcome*	
Gather In My Name Event 1 Distribution of keepsake books, heart or cross medallions, and parent information	
Send Parent Letter 2: *Readiness*	Parents and guardians teach Sessions 1 to 4 from **keepsake books** using detailed lesson plans in **First Penance** or **First Communion Guide** or **Home Lesson Plans**. Parents assist children in developing scrapbook pages and work on the "Family Time" pages from the **First Penance** or **First Communion Guide**
Gather In My Name Event 2	
Option: Individual Readiness Meetings between the pastor or his delegate and each child and parent	Parents and guardians teach sessions 5 and 6, review chapters, assist with scrapbook pages, work on the "Family Time" pages from the **First Penance** or **First Communion Guide**, and discern readiness of their children to receive sacrament
Rehearsal and celebration of First Penance or First Communion	

Forming Catechists and Volunteers

Once you have established your model for the preparation process, you will need to recruit catechists and other volunteers for the program. If you offer Model 1 or Model 2, you will need catechists for the parish-based sessions.

Review the preparation sections of all four *Gather In My Name* events in this guide to determine how much additional help you will need. The size of your group of volunteers for set up, clean up, and other roles will depend on how many people you expect to take part in the events. Though it is advisable, it is not absolutely necessary to have catechists at the *Gather In My Name* events, as all activities employ self-directed interaction in small groups.

Involving Families

Clear and consistent communication with families helps them to take responsibility for their child's sacramental preparation. www.webelieveandcelebrate.com offers a family section with *Home Lesson Plans*, scrapbooking project cards, eCards and more. Check the web site frequently, as it is updated regularly.

Parent Letters

We Believe & Celebrate provides letters to send to parents and guardians for each of the sacraments. Owners of this manual may download templates from our www.webelieveandcelebrate.com and customize them to include information about your program. There are two letters for each sacrament.

- Parent Letter 1: *Welcome* gives an overview of the process, plus an invitation to the first *Gather In My Name* event.

- Parent Letter 2: *Readiness* helps parents discern their child's preparedness to receive each sacrament. It also invites them to the second *Gather In My Name* event.

If your candidates will receive the Sacraments of Initiation in the Proper Order (Confirmation and then Eucharist), we offer alternative versions of the Parent Letters on our web site.

Making Memories with Scrapbooking

Scrapbooking is a fun way to relive major events in the life of a family. It is also a way of sharing experiences, telling stories, and expressing ideas and feelings. Scrapbooking is a major feature of *We Believe & Celebrate*. In each keepsake book, children and families can use intricate scrapbooking techniques or simply use pens, markers, and wax pencils to complete the activities in the *We Gather* and *We Respond* sections. They can also preserve and share their most cherished drawings, photographs, journaling, and quotations (and the memories behind them) by scrapbooking these pages. During each of the *Gather In My Name* events, participants will make parish scrapbook pages for your entire faith community to enjoy. You will need to provide two scapbooks, or binders, for the *Gather In My Name* events. Designate one for the two First Penance events and the other for the two First Communion events.

You can add new pages to these scrapbooks each year, or create new scrapbooks for each group preparing for First Penance or First Communion. Either way, these scrapbooks will become a treasured part of your parish archives.

At www.webelieveandcelebrate.com you will find the following scrapbooking aids:

- project cards for each chapter's *We Gather* and *We Respond* pages

- stencils and sticker art

- handouts and scrapbooking pages to use as part of the *Gather In My Name* events.

We Believe & Celebrate First Penance

Components in this Section of the Guide

Getting Started (pages 9–10)
These pages will help you get organized. Here and at www.webelieveandcelebrate.com you will find all you need to begin as well as additional resources.

Two *Gather In My Name* Events (pages 11–34)
Developed as an alternative to the conventional parent meeting, these intergenerational sessions draw your entire parish community into the preparation process.

Event 1, "Forgiving Hearts," uses the Scripture story of the Prodigal Son to explore the love and forgiveness of God and brings this forgiveness into the participants' daily lives.

Event 2, "Go in Peace," presents the order of the Rite of Penance and leads participants to appreciate the peace they receive in their hearts and share with others through the sacrament.

Participants at these two events will make a parish keepsake—a treasury of faith statements and prayers your parish community can cherish year after year.

Setting the Schedule

Many parishes celebrate First Penance as a communal celebration with individual confession and absolution for each child. Individual celebrations with the priest are usually provided for children who cannot be part of the communal celebration. Some parishes encourage children to celebrate First Penance individually during the parish's regularly scheduled hours for the Sacrament of Penance and Reconciliation.

No matter which option you choose, strive to make it a true celebration and a joyful acknowledgement of the grace we receive through this sacrament. Consider these questions: How will the celebration of First Penance draw the children, their families, and the greater community into the sacramental life of the Church? How will the celebration inspire lifelong love for the Sacrament of Penance?

Start by establishing the date(s) for the children's first reception of the Sacrament of Penance. If you offer multiple celebrations, establish the date for the first one. Work backwards from there to set dates for the rest of the program. Download a timetable at our web site.

Getting Started

Involving Parents and Guardians

Parents and guardians play a primary role in the faith development of their children. *We Believe & Celebrate First Penance* promotes parental involvement through textbooks, lesson plans, and tools to help parents journey with their child toward celebrating this sacrament.

Parent Letters

Owners of this manual may download parent letter templates from www.webelieveandcelebrate.com and customize them to include specific program information. There are two letters for First Penance:

Parent Letter 1: *Welcome* gives an overview of the process, plus an invitation to the first *Gather In My Name* event. It includes a sample program schedule and a short article on discerning readiness for the sacrament throughout the preparation period.

Parent Letter 2: *Readiness* invites parents and guardians into the final preparation for the sacrament and reminds them of the second *Gather In My Name* event. If you choose to offer Readiness Meetings, this letter also provides that invitation.

Readiness Meeting for First Penance *(Optional)*

In the last few weeks before the celebration you might want to schedule Readiness Meetings. These conversations between the pastor or his delegate, the children, and their parents build excitement for the celebration of the Sacrament of Penance. They also give parents and guardians further input as to how ready their children are to receive the Sacrament of Penance. This is not an interview or a final exam, but a discernment process.

In the case of a very large group, the pastor may wish to have multiple facilitators of these meetings, including members of the parish staff or clergy. However, be sure that the facilitator of the meeting is someone who can directly answer families' concerns or questions about the sacrament, their children's readiness, and the program.

The meeting need not be long. We suggest a relaxed format with three simple parts:

1. **Gathering.** Welcome the family, offer light refreshments, and ask the child non-threatening questions about school, a recent holiday, or some favorite activities. Ask if the child has enjoyed the preparation process, and invite the child to show you favorite pages from the keepsake book.

2. **What happens during the rite?** Tell the child that you would like to talk about what he or she has been learning about the Sacrament of Penance. Open the child's keepsake book to page 60 in Chapter 5: "We Celebrate Penance with the Church." Draw the child's attention to the first paragraph, describing the communal celebration of the Sacrament of Penance. Review the parts and provide an outline of what his or her celebration will be like. Invite the child to look at the photos and text on pages 62 and 63. Talk about the way the child can receive this sacrament again and again throughout his or her life, either individually or with the community. Ask the child if he or she has any questions about the rite.

3. **Receiving the sacrament.** Remind the child that you are excited that he or she is getting ready to celebrate the Sacrament of Penance. Turn to page 72 in the keepsake book and have the child look over the photo and words. Then ask, "What happens to us through the Sacrament of Penance?" Affirm all of the correct answers, including those on the page: we are filled with God's grace; we are joined to God and the Church; God takes away punishment for our sins; we receive peace and comfort; we are strengthened to love God. Ask the child how he or she feels about all of these gifts from God. Ask if there is anything he or she is wondering about or is concerned about regarding the Sacrament of Penance. Discuss these things together.

In the final few moments, invite the parents or guardians to share any concerns or questions. If they raise concerns about the child's readiness, or if you have concerns, you may choose to speak with them privately. This is a good time to share any last minute information about the upcoming celebration.

If you are planning to present the children with certificates after they celebrate the Sacrament of Penance, complete them after the Readiness Meetings are held. To order certificates, visit www.sadlier.com/catalog.

ONLINE COMPONENTS
Visit www.webelieveandcelebrate.com

First Penance Event 1

Leader's Guide **Forgiving Hearts**

Objectives

To learn the four parts of the Sacrament of Penance: contrition, confession, a penance, and absolution

To understand how the parable of the Prodigal Son (Luke 15:11–32) parallels the Church's celebration of the Sacrament of Penance

To identify ways we can be more forgiving of one another in order to live Jesus' example of love and forgiveness

To offer our support to the children who are preparing to celebrate the Sacrament of Penance for the first time

Faith Response

Participants will be able to name the four parts of the Sacrament of Penance and to identify ways to expand their own capacity to seek and extend forgiveness.

Source Material

✦ Sadlier *We Believe & Celebrate First Penance*

✦ Sadlier Faith and Witness *Liturgy and Worship: A Course on Prayer and Sacraments*

✦ Schlabach, Joetta Handrich. *Extending the Table: A World Community Cookbook.* Pennsylvania: Herald Press, 1991.

✦ Bishops' Committee on the Liturgy. *Catholic Household Blessings and Prayers.* Washington, D.C.: United States Catholic Conference of Bishops, 1991.

Format Choice	GIMN Option 1	GIMN Option 2
What is it?	full multigenerational event	multigenerational event with breakout sessions
Who participates?	adults, children, and youth together for the entire session	adults, children, and youth come together for opening activities, then children break out into cluster groups
How do I follow this guide?	complete everything **except** the "Option 2 Only" tabs	complete everything **except** the "Option 1 Only" tabs for adults and youth; children's breakout session outlines online
What are the benefits?	the entire parish community partakes in the event together	expansive presentation for adults and older youth; age-appropriate presentation for First Communion, Confirmation, and Proper Order candidates

Outline and Notes

Background for Leaders and Adults

The Sacrament of Penance celebrates our continuing conversion, our turning from selfishness and sin to love and generosity in order to fully embrace God's love and forgiveness. This sacrament is meant to help us to heal what is broken and to set free that which is bound up. This sacrament is not only for the times when we commit serious, or mortal, sin. Whenever we confess our venial sins we are strengthened and grow in God's grace. This is why young children, most likely incapable of serious sin at this point in their lives, are called to the sacrament. It introduces them to a lifelong process of self-examination in which they are called to wholeness and maturity by responding to the love God has shown us in Christ Jesus.

Option 1 Multigenerational Event

Option 2 Multigenerational Event with Breakout Sessions

Before We Gather

Publicity

Publicizing the event is an important component of preparation. Visit www.webelieveandcelebrate.com for resources.

Preparation

To prepare for this *Gather In My Name* (*GIMN*) event, you, the leader, are encouraged to read over all the material and familiarize yourself with the content and the process. The following guidelines will help you in preparing for the event. Download handouts and a preparation chart at our web site.

Preparing the Gathering Space

◆ Set up enough tables that seat eight to ten people to accommodate your group.

◆ Arrange childcare for children under the age of four.

Option 2 Only

◆ Arrange a space for the breakout group meetings. Recruit a catechist to lead each breakout group. Download breakout session outlines at our web site.

◆ Set up a focal point for prayer. Spread a table with a decorative cloth of the appropriate liturgical color. Set up stands to display the Bible and the scrapbook you will use for the two Penance *Gather In My Name* events in this guide.

◆ Review the opening prayer on pages 16 and 17. Obtain a purple shawl or cloth to use as the mantle in the reading of the Prodigal

Son. Beside the prayer table, set a chair or easel on which to drape the mantle.

◆ Leave a space in front of the prayer table for acting out the Gospel story during the opening prayer.

◆ Purchase a heart medallion or other keepsake for each child preparing for the first reception of the Sacrament of Penance. To order heart medallions visit www.sadlier.com/catalog. Place the keepsakes in a basket on the prayer table.

◆ Read "Lost and Found" (handout #3). Hide the following five items in various spots around the room: a Bible, a large candle, the purple mantle, a heart medallion, and the scrapbook.

◆ Make copies of the following handouts:

  • for each person: table blessing (handout #2); "The Prodigal Son" (handout #4)

  • for each household: recipe (handout #1); "Lost and Found" (handout #3); "Forgiving Hearts" (handout #10)

  • For each table: scrapbook pages (handout #6); "I Want to Be More Forgiving" (handout #7). You may need to provide more than one scrapbook page to each table, so have extra copies available. **Option:** Purchase and use your own scrapbook pages in place of handout #6.

  • for children and adults as needed: children's activity sheets (handout #9); evaluation forms (handout #8)

◆ Make copies of "Family Letters" (handout #5), so that each table receives a different letter: #5A, #5B, #5C, or #5D. If there are more than four tables, assign the same letter to more than one group.

◆ Make six copies of handout #12 for the volunteers who will pantomime the Prodigal Son parable during the opening prayer.

◆ Assemble a basket of scrapbooking supplies for each table. Each basket should include pens, pencils, markers, scissors, tape, adhesive, and colored paper or tagboard. Include other items as desired, such as ribbon, string, glitter, or buttons.

◆ Before the event, ask households to bring photographs of family members who will attend. These photos will be pasted into a parish keepsake and should be photos that can be left at the parish.

◆ Invite representatives from groups such as the Knights of Columbus, Altar and Rosary Society, pastoral council, Confirmation candidates, or other parish groups to take part in the event by presenting keepsakes and personal letters to the children during the closing prayer. Send these groups copies of handout #11, which explains the process in more detail.

✦ If you will distribute the *We Believe & Celebrate First Penance* keepsake books to the children preparing for the Sacrament of Penance, set these books near the prayer table.

Getting Started

Seat two to three households at each table, including those who are attending as individuals.

As participants enter, give each a copy of "Lost and Found" (handout #3). Invite them to search for the hidden items.

Recruit six volunteers to pantomime the story of the Prodigal Son during the opening prayer. You will need the following characters: the father, two sons, two friends and a servant. **Option:** If there are older children preparing for Penance, you might ask them to play these roles. Provide the actors with a copy of the script and prompts (handout #12).

If you will use the *We Believe & Celebrate First Penance/First Communion Music CD*, set up a CD player.

When We Gather

Meal Plan *(Optional)*

To build a greater sense of community, plan a festive meal before or after the event. Here are some ideas to consider as you plan:

✦ Host a "Salad and Spuds" meal. Provide large bowls of salad greens and baked potatoes. Invite households to bring a salad or potato topping such as chopped vegetables or meat, grated cheese, croutons, or salsa.

✦ Prepare batches of sesame seed cookies (handout #1). Cut the cookies into heart shapes.

✦ Offer a table blessing (handout #2).

Opening/Ice-Breaker *10 minutes*

Lost and Found

✦ After everyone has had a chance to search for the hidden items, convene the group by asking households to take their places at the tables.

✦ Elicit responses to the "Lost and Found" activity. As items are found, retrieve them and place them on different tables.

✦ Ask participants to share how they felt while searching for the items. Ask how they felt when they found an item.

✦ Invite the tables to choose someone from their group to carry the item at their table to the prayer table during the opening prayer.

Session Overview *5 minutes*

✦ Introduce the session with the following points:

- In this *Gather In My Name* event we will listen to a story that Jesus told about a lost and found son. This story reminds us that we have choices to make if we want to follow God's law of love.

- Through the Sacrament of Penance we are forgiven for the choices we have made that turn us away from God's love. We are able to find our way back to God who is always ready to forgive us if we are truly sorry.

✦ Ask the children who are preparing for the sacrament to stand. Note what a special time this is for them. Explain that, as members of their parish community, we want them to know that they can always turn to God who loves and forgives them.

✦ Add housekeeping and other announcements.

✦ The pastor might offer a brief word of welcome at this time.

✦ Ask those who will carry the lost items during the prayer to bring them to the back of the room.

✦ Distribute copies of "The Prodigal Son" (handout #4) and invite the groups to ready themselves for prayer.

Opening Prayer: The Prodigal Son *10 minutes*

The GIMN leader or the pastor serves as the leader of the opening prayer.

All stand.

Leader: Let us sing our opening song,
"A Circle of Love."
(*We Believe & Celebrate First Penance/First Communion Music CD* #10)

Chorus:
A circle of love, yes a circle of love;
each hand in a hand, a circle of friends.
A circle of love that is open to all;
we open the circle and welcome each one of you in.

1. Each person has something to bring:
   a song, a story, a smile, a teardrop, a dream,
   and loving to share. (Chorus)

2. Jesus calls us to come close to him;
   the tall, the smaller, the young, the older,
   with colors so rich and so rare. (Chorus)

3. All people are special to God:
   the lost, the lonely, the sick, the hungry.
   With God now we welcome them in. (Chorus)

As the group sings, the items for the prayer table are brought forward.
All make the sign of the cross.

Leader: Let us come with confidence before the throne of grace
to receive God's mercy,
and we shall find pardon and strength in our time of need.
Blessed be God for ever.

All: Blessed be God for ever.
(*Catholic Household Blessings and Prayers*)

Leader: Let us listen now to a story about a son who left home, a father
who welcomed him back, and a brother who had a hard time
forgiving.

All sit.

Those who will play the characters for the story come forward. Read the story,
pausing between lines while the characters pantomime the actions.

Leader: This is a story based on the Gospel of Luke 15:11–32.

There was a loving father who had two sons.

One day the younger son asked for his share of the family's
money.

The father gave it to him, and the son left home.

The son spent all of his money with his friends. And when the money was gone, his friends left him.

He had nowhere to live and no money to buy clothes or food.

The son thought about his selfish choices. He remembered his father's love. He decided to go home and ask his father for forgiveness.

When the young man was almost home, his father saw him on the road. The father ran out to welcome his son.

The young man said, "Father, I have sinned against heaven and against you; I no longer deserve to be called your son" (Luke 15:21).

The father was very happy to see his son. He called for his servant to bring a robe to replace the son's ragged clothes.

Then the father gathered his family and friends for a celebration.

The older son was coming home from his work in the fields. He heard the music and saw the dancing.

The older son called his father's servant and asked what was happening. The servant told him about the return of the younger son.

The older son became very angry and refused to go inside.

His father came outside and began to plead with him. "My son, you are here with me always; everything I have is yours. But now we must celebrate and rejoice, because your brother . . . was lost and has been found." (Luke 15:31–32)

The Gospel of the Lord.

All: Praise to you, Lord Jesus Christ.

Pause while the characters return to their seats.

All stand.

Leader: Lord God, you ask us to love you and to love each other as we love ourselves. Sometimes we make choices that lead us away from that love. When we are lost, help us to find our way back home to you. We ask this in the name of Jesus Christ, through the power of the Holy Spirit.

All: Amen.

Writing Some Family Letters *30 minutes*

Option 2 Only

Age Group Gatherings *5 minutes*
✦ After the opening prayer, divide the children into breakout groups with the catechists who will lead the breakout group sessions.

✦ Recall the Gospel story from the opening prayer. Ask these or similar questions and elicit the responses that follow them:

- What made the younger son return home? (He realized he had made selfish choices.) What did he say to the father when he came home? (He apologized and asked for forgiveness.) What did the father do? (He forgave the son and gathered the family for a celebration.) How did the older brother react to his father's decision? (He was angry and did not want to be part of the celebration.)

✦ Point out that the father reminds us of God who is always ready to forgive us and welcome us home, even when we make selfish choices.

✦ Invite the groups to use their imaginations to explore the parable.

Option 1 Only

✦ Distribute "Family Letters" (handout #5). Give each table group a different letter: #5A, #5B, #5C, or #5D. If there are more than four tables, assign the same letter to multiple groups.

✦ Allow time for the groups to complete the letters.

Option 2 Only

✦ Distribute "Family Letters" (handouts #5B and #5D). Give handout #5B to half of the table groups and handout #5D to the other half. These handouts are letters from the father to his sons. Children in breakout sessions will complete handouts #5A and #5C, letters from the sons to their father.

✦ Allow time for the groups to complete the letters. Use any remaining time to review the sacrament.

✦ Help the children rejoin their table groups as they return.

✦ Ask volunteers to read the letters aloud. Start with the letter from the younger son (handout #5A) and the father's response (handout #5B). End with the letter from the older son (handout #5C) and the father's response (handout #5D).

✦ After all of the letters have been read, lead the groups in a round of applause for their creativity and insights.

✦ In these or your own words, draw out the following points.

- When the younger son left home, he may have felt excited at first. But then he began to feel sad about the poor choices he had made. He was sorry and did not want to act this way again. This is called *contrition*.

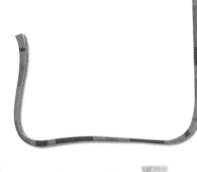

- When he returned home, the younger son told his father he was sorry. He told his father about the selfish and hurtful choices he had made. This is called *confession*.

- The younger son was willing to do whatever he needed to do to show his sorrow and to make up for his selfish choices. A prayer or kind act that we do to show God we are sorry is called *a penance*.

- The father forgave his son and even had a celebration for him. In the Sacrament of Penance, God forgives our sins through the words and actions of the priest. This is called *absolution*.

- When the older son came home and found a party going on he felt angry and hurt. He refused to attend. It seemed unfair to him, and maybe to us, too. The father reassured his older son that he was loved. The father also encouraged his older son to be forgiving and not angry and resentful.

Break *10 minutes*

Making a Parish Keepsake *30 minutes*

I Want to be More Forgiving

✦ Introduce the activity with these or similar words:

- In the letters we shared, many feelings were expressed: hurt, anger, sorrow, and contrition. We heard words of love and forgiveness. Listen again and imagine just for a moment that they are the words of our loving God to you—God speaking to your heart.

✦ Reread one of the moving sentences from a group who completed a letter from the father. Allow a moment for those words to sink in.

✦ Ask the participants to reflect on the following questions:

- How does it feel to hear how much God loves you? to know that God forgives you when you are truly sorry, no matter what you have said or done? How might we forgive others as God has forgiven us?

✦ Distribute scrapbook pages (handout #6) and directions (handout #7). Invite the groups to scrapbook their pages using the family photos they brought or an appropriate symbol or drawing.

✦ Ask each table to compose a short prayer and place it in the center of the page. Designate someone at each table to read it during the closing prayer.

✦ Distribute evaluations (handout #8) and children's activity sheets (handout #9) for participants to complete after the activity.

Wrap-up *5 minutes*

✦ Distribute copies of "Forgiving Hearts" (handout #10) and the recipe for sesame seed cookies (handout #1).

✦ If time permits, elicit feedback from the group about this event. Ask the participants what they learned about God's gift of forgiveness.

Closing Prayer *10 minutes*

Invite the participants to quiet themselves for prayer. Ask them to look at their scrapbook pages and to reflect on the following questions: What do you notice about the ways we share forgiveness with others? Take a moment to admire the pages of tables around you. What do you see? How do you feel?

If time allows, invite short responses from the group. After sharing, invite all to stand and sing the refrain and first verse from "A Circle of Love."

***Option:** Have a live musician continue playing the song quietly behind the spoken parts.*

Leader: God of forgiveness,
You are the loving Father,
who waits for us,
watches for us,
longs for us to return.

Whether we go far away
like the Prodigal Son,
or stay close by your side like his brother,
you are constant.
You are faithful to us.
You give us all that you have.
You love us.
You ask us to love others in the same way,
without any condition.
No matter what.
No matter what!

God of forgiveness,
we raise our hearts to you
with praise and thanksgiving,
with petition,
with intercession
as we offer our litany of forgiveness.

Invite everyone to respond "God of forgiveness, we pray to you" after each prayer. Representatives should come forward, read their prayers, place their scrapbook pages in or near the scrapbook on the prayer table and return to their seats. After all the prayers have been offered, continue.

Leader: Grateful to God
for the forgiveness he has shown us
we pray for those young people
beginning the journey toward
the Sacrament of Penance.
I ask each of the children
preparing for the sacrament
to stand and receive this gift as a sign of God's love for you.
May your upcoming celebration of the Sacrament of Penance
bring you peace.

Invited or parish representatives or parents take one of the heart medallions or keepsakes from the prayer table and present it to their selected candidate. They offer good wishes from the parish community, place the medallion around the child's neck, and then offer the child a Sign of Peace. The representatives remain standing next to the candidates for the closing blessing. When all have completed the ritual, continue.

Leader: Dear Children,
we rejoice in how much God our Father loves you and calls you to be his own. Now, as your own family and your family the Church, we raise our hands in blessing.

Invite all to raise their hands in blessing toward the children. Parents place their hands on their child's head or shoulder. Ask the group to echo the words of the blessing after each line.

Leader: We bless your name, O God,
you who made us and love us.
And breathed us into being.
Bless these children of yours,
called to share in this sacrament
with healing, forgiveness, and peace,
with the gift of your unbounded love,
and the courage to always return to you.
In Jesus Christ, your Son, through the power of the Holy Spirit,
we pray, Amen!
Our celebration is ended.
Let us go forth to love and serve the Lord.

All: Thanks be to God.

Song: "A Circle of Love"

Outline and Notes

(One day to two weeks after the event)

Follow-up is an important part of the *Gather In My Name* process. Here are some ideas for tying up loose ends and looking ahead to future events:

- ✦ If you did not use the evaluation form at the end of the event, send it to participants one to two weeks later. Completed forms will provide feedback about the ways participants applied what was shared to their lives and help you in planning future events.

- ✦ Share your experience with the *Gather In My Name* writing team. As an individual or planning team, complete the feedback form and email it to webeditor@sadlier.com. If desired, send digital pictures of your event. We will email you a permissions form if we would like to use your photos on our web site.

- ✦ If you used the children's activity sheets during or after the session, you might want to set up a display where parishioners can view them. Do this one to two weeks after the event to help the rest of the parish learn about the sacramental preparation process.

- ✦ Place copies of "Forgiving Hearts" (handout #10) in the bulletin or provide a link to it on the parish web site.

- ✦ Keep the parish keepsake scrapbook album in a visible place throughout the preparation process. Add pages by including copies of special bulletins, fliers, and prayer sheets along with short journaling pieces that explain what is going on. Take pictures of the children and their families as they gather for catechetical sessions and parish liturgies and make a page about each one.

- ✦ Create a link to www.webelieveandcelebrate.com on your parish web site. Invite the children who attended the *Gather In My Name* event to send an eCard from this site to someone who has taught them what it means to be a forgiving person.

FIRST PENANCE EVENT 2

Leader's Guide Go In Peace

Objectives

To understand that the Sacrament of Penance is a journey of faith and forgiveness

To be reminded that when we ask God to forgive us, we receive the great gift of peace

To turn to God with our whole hearts, in order to become peacemakers for the entire world

Faith Response

Participants will be able to to name ways to be peacemakers within their communities.

Source Material

✦ Sadlier *We Believe & Celebrate First Penance*

✦ Sadlier Faith and Witness *Liturgy and Worship: A Course on Prayer and Sacraments*

✦ Bishops' Committee on the Liturgy. *Catholic Household Blessings and Prayers.* Washington, D.C.: United States Catholic Conference of Bishops, 1991.

✦ Curry, Rick. *The Secrets of Jesuit Soupmaking: A Year of Our Soups.* New York: Penguin, 2002.

Format

Gather In My Name is a full multigenerational event of approximately ninety minutes with the optional inclusion of a meal. First Penance Event 2 is designed to reinforce the concepts presented in Chapter 5 of the *We Believe & Celebrate First Penance* keepsake book. It is recommended that this event be scheduled just before or after the presentation of that lesson.

Outline and Notes

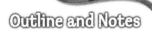

Background for Leaders and Adults

When celebrating the Sacrament of Penance individually or with the community, there is an introductory or gathering experience that welcomes us and draws us into the community of faith. Ideally, we enter the rite with a contrite heart, having reflected upon the sins that have fractured our relationships with particular people, with the community of faith, with God, and with ourselves. By confessing our sins, we let go of the shame, embarrassment, regret, and resentment that prevent us from responding to God's love. Absolution is the central prayer of the sacrament, and it includes a declaration of God's forgiveness that conveys both pardon and peace. In taking on a penance, we resolve to open ourselves further to the love of God in Jesus Christ through prayer and acts of love, service, kindness, and compassion. We are then sent forth, strengthened by the grace of God and ready to share the peace of the sacrament with others.

Before We Gather

Publicity

Publicizing the event is an important component of preparation. Visit www.webelieveandcelebrate.com for resources.

Preparation

To prepare for this event, you, the leader, are encouraged to read over all the material and familiarize yourself with the content and the process. The following guidelines will help you in preparing for the event. Download handouts and a preparation chart at our web site.

Preparing the Gathering Space

- ✦ Set up enough tables that seat eight to ten people to accommodate your group.

- ✦ Arrange childcare for children under the age of four.

- ✦ Set up a focal point for prayer. Spread a table with a decorative cloth of the appropriate liturgical color. Set up stands to display the Bible and the scrapbook assembled in the "Forgiving Hearts" *GIMN* event. The following items will be carried to the prayer table during the opening prayer: the Bible, scrapbook, a large candle, and a heart medallion. Keep these items on a table in the back of the room. If a processional cross is available, set the stand in front of the prayer table and keep the cross with the other items.

- ✦ Make one copy of handout #5 on colored construction paper. Cut it out and affix it to a page from the parish keepsake scrapbook album. Place it with the processional items.

◆ Read over the opening prayer.

◆ If you will use the *We Believe & Celebrate First Penance/First Communion Music CD*, set up a CD player.

◆ Recruit two volunteers to read the parts in the story of the Penitent Woman. Give each a copy of handout #11 and encourage them to be expressive and creative in their rendition of the story. **Option:** Invite members of a parish youth group to read the parts. Make the reading more dramatic by asking volunteers to wear costumes and memorize their parts.

◆ Make copies of the following handouts:

- for each person: table blessing (handout #2); "The Penitent Woman" (handout #4); "Symbols of Peace" (handout #7)

- for each household: recipe (handout #1); "Go In Peace" (handout #10)

- for each table: "Heart Stuff" (handout #3); heart outline (handout #5)

- for children and adults as needed: children's activity sheets (handout #9); evaluation forms (handout #8)

◆ Assemble a large basket of cookies, candy, or other goodies to use as the prize for the "Heart Stuff" activity. Make sure there are enough goodies for the entire group.

◆ Purchase a large piece of poster board for each table.

◆ Read over "The Heart of the Sacrament" activity and determine whether to hang the groups' posters on the walls or position them on easels.

◆ Make copies of "The Heart of the Sacrament" (handout #6) so that each table receives a different page: #6A, #6B, #6C, or #6D. If there are more than four tables, assign the same page to multiple groups.

◆ Assemble a basket of scrapbooking supplies for each table. Each basket should include pens, pencils, markers, scissors, masking tape, and a stapler. Include other embellishment items as desired, such as ribbon, string, glitter, and glue.

◆ When you send families information about the event, ask the children preparing for the Sacrament of Penance to wear the heart medallions they received at the "Forgiving Hearts" event.

◆ **Option:** Present copies of *With Jesus Always* to each child preparing for First Penance as a special gift. See www.sadlier.com/catalog for ordering information.

Getting Started

After participants enter and register, invite them to be seated at one of the tables. Seat two to three households at each table, including those who are attending as individuals.

Recruit volunteers to carry the Bible, scrapbook, candle, heart scrapbook page, and processional cross to the prayer table during the opening prayer.

When We Gather

Meal Plan *(Optional)*

To build a greater sense of community, plan a festive meal before or after the event. Here are some ideas to consider as you plan:

✦ Plan an international theme by making a large batch of Vietnamese chicken salad (handout #1). Invite each household to bring a dish that represents a different culture or country. Decorate tables with signs that say *peace* in different languages.

✦ Ask different parish groups to sponsor a meal for the event as a way to show their love and support for the children and their families.

✦ Offer a table blessing (handout #2).

Opening/Ice-Breaker *10 minutes*

Heart Stuff

✦ Give each table a copy of "Heart Stuff" (handout #3).

✦ Ask each table to appoint a recorder.

✦ Explain that you will give the groups one minute to write as many phrases that have the word *heart* in them as possible. After one minute, the table with the most phrases recorded on their handout will win a prize.

✦ When all are ready, start the activity. At the end of sixty seconds, ask each table to stop and tally their phrases.

✦ Ask the winning table to call out their phrases. Invite other tables to add phrases to their lists.

✦ Award the prize basket to the winning table and invite the winners to share their bounty with the rest of the tables!

✦ **Option:** Instead of awarding a prize after the first round, do it after a second round using the word *peace*.

Session Overview *5 minutes*

✦ Introduce the session by drawing out the following points:

- In this *Gather In My Name* event we will learn how the Sacrament of Penance is a wonderful journey of the heart.

- We will hear a story about a woman who came to Jesus for forgiveness. This story reminds us of the great gift of peace we receive when we ask God to forgive us.

- The Sacrament of Penance gives us God's gift of peace when we turn to God with our whole hearts. With our hearts filled with peace, we can become peacemakers in our families, our communities, and the world.

✦ Acknowledge the children who are preparing to celebrate the Sacrament of Penance. Remind them that the parish community continues to pray for them.

✦ Add housekeeping and other announcements.

✦ The pastor might offer a brief word of welcome at this time.

✦ Distribute copies of "The Penitent Woman" (handout #4) and invite the groups to ready themselves for prayer.

Opening Prayer: The Penitent Woman *10 minutes*

The GIMN leader or the pastor serves as the leader of the opening prayer. As the group sings, the items for the prayer table are brought forward, starting with the processional cross.

All Stand.

Leader: Please join in our opening song, "Open Our Hearts."
(*We Believe & Celebrate First Penance/First Communion Music CD #17*)

1. God, we come to worship you:
Open our hearts to listen to you.
Open our hearts to listen to you.

2. God, you made us, we are yours:
Open our hearts to listen to you.
Open our hearts to listen to you.

3. God, your love is always true:
Open our hearts to listen to you.
Open our hearts to listen to you.

4. Faithful God, we trust in you:
Open our hearts to listen to you.
Open our hearts to listen to you.

All make the sign of the cross.

Leader: Let us come with confidence before the throne of grace
to receive God's mercy,
and we shall find pardon and strength in our time of need.
Blessed be God for ever.

All: Blessed be God for ever.
(*Catholic Household Blessings and Prayers*)

All sit.

Leader: We will now hear a story based on Luke 7:36–50 about a woman who sinned and was sorry. One day she learned that Jesus was visiting the home of a rich man named Simon. Listen to what both of them learned about forgiveness.

Ask the readers to come forward.

Woman: I had heard Jesus was visiting at the house of Simon the Pharisee. I had to try to see him. I had purchased a gift for him, an alabaster flask of perfumed ointment. I was determined to bring it to him.

Simon: It was wonderful to have Jesus, the renowned preacher from Galilee, at my house. I had set a fine dinner for him. As we ate, we talked about the Reign of God. What an amazing gift Jesus has for storytelling! It was all so enjoyable—until that woman barged in to see Jesus.

Woman: When I got up the courage to go into the house, I ran to Jesus. I planned to give him the gift and leave, but I found myself frozen in place standing before him. I tried to tell Jesus of my admiration for him but I couldn't speak.

I felt hot tears on my face and an overwhelming sense of God's love coming from him. I met his gaze, just for an instant, and felt his unquestioning acceptance.

Simon: What was this woman doing in my house? And what was her business with Jesus? Why did he look at her so calmly, and say nothing? Surely, if he were a prophet, he would know that she is a public sinner!

Woman: With that one look, I knew why I had come. My tears flowed freely now, with love for him and for God, and also with sorrow for my sins and for everything that had kept me from loving God. My tears fell like rain on Jesus' feet. I dried his feet with my hair, kissed them, and anointed them with the perfumed oil.

Simon: My thoughts must have shown on my face, for Jesus interrupted them. He said, "Two people were in debt to a certain creditor; one owed five hundred days' wages and the other owed fifty. Since they were unable to repay the debt, he forgave it for both. Which of them will love him more?" (Luke 7:41–42). I answered, "The one, I suppose, whose larger debt was forgiven" (Luke 7:43).

Woman: Jesus said, "You have judged rightly" (Luke 7:43). He turned to me and said, "Do you see this woman? When I entered your house, you did not give me water for my feet, but she has bathed them with her tears and wiped them with her hair. You did not give me a kiss, but she has not ceased kissing my feet. . . . You did not anoint my head with oil, but she anointed my feet with ointment. So I tell you, her many sins have been forgiven; hence, she has shown great love" (Luke 7:44–47). And then he turned to me with eyes full of love and said, "Your sins are forgiven. . . . Your faith has saved you; go in peace" (Luke 7:48, 50).

Leader: The Gospel of the Lord.

All: Praise to you, Lord Jesus Christ.

Pause while the characters return to their seats.

All stand.

Leader: Lord God,
even before we think of turning to you,
you love us more than we can imagine.
You want to help us, to make us whole, to forgive our sins.
Open our hearts to your unconditional love.
Lead us on the path of forgiveness
that will bring us to your peace.
We ask this through Christ Jesus, our Lord.

All: Amen.

The Heart of the Sacrament *35 minutes*

✦ Recall the Gospel story from the opening prayer. Ask about Jesus' final words to the woman.

- What did Jesus say to the woman who washed his feet with her tears? ("Your sins are forgiven. . . . Your faith has saved you. Go in peace." [Luke 7:48, 50])

- Imagine that you are the woman at Jesus' feet. How might you have felt after Jesus said these things? (relieved? happy?)

- What do you think the woman learned about forgiveness? (that God's forgiveness brings peace; that God loves and forgives us.)

- What do you think Simon might have learned about forgiveness? (Hopefully, he learned not to judge people and that God extends forgiveness in ways we may not understand.)

✦ Reiterate the last thing Jesus said to the woman: "Go in peace." Suggest that the woman might have felt peaceful after Jesus spoke to her because Jesus wished her peace.

- We believe that when we receive the gift of God's forgiveness through the Sacrament of Penance, it helps us to find peace with God and with each other. This is our hope for all of the young people who are receiving the Sacrament of Penance for the first time. We pray that celebrating the sacrament will make us happy and peaceful.

✦ Distribute one copy of the heart outline (handout #5) to each table. Distribute "The Heart of the Sacrament" (handout #6). Give each table group a different page: #6A, #6B, #6C, or #6D. If there are more than four tables, assign the same page to multiple groups. Distribute a piece of blank poster board to each table.

✦ Invite the groups to read the directions and to complete the posters. Stress that each person at the table should take part in the activity.

✦ Allow time for the groups to complete the poster. Circulate from table to table to offer help as needed. Remind the groups to complete the prayer exercise and to choose someone to read it during the closing prayer.

✦ After all of the posters have been completed, invite the recorder from each table to share an explanation of the group's poster. Then invite everyone to take a break.

✦ During the break, display the posters on the walls or on easels. Space them about six feet apart and in sequential order.

Break *10 minutes*

The Peace of the Sacrament *15 minutes*

✦ Point out that the Sacrament of Penance is often called the Sacrament of Reconciliation or the Sacrament of Peace.

+ Use these or similar words to explain the effects of the sacrament:

  • The last words that Jesus said to the woman in the story were, "Your faith has saved you; go in peace" (Luke 7:50).

  • When we confess our sins, we can let go of feeling sad or embarrassed or guilty. We are then free to respond to God's love.

  • The Sacrament of Penance offers us forgiveness and pardon for our sins and fills us with peace. These are called the effects of the sacrament and all of them are mentioned in the prayer of absolution offered by the priest in the Sacrament of Penance:

  "God, the Father of mercies,
  through the death and resurrection of his Son
  has reconciled the world to himself
  and sent the Holy Spirit among us
  for the forgiveness of sins;
  through the ministry of the Church
  may God give you pardon and peace,
  and I absolve you from your sins
  in the name of the Father, and of the Son, †
  and of the Holy Spirit." (The Rite of Penance)

  • Like the woman in Luke's Gospel, we can take this peace out into the world and share it with others.

+ Ask participants to consider how they will bring peace to others. Distribute a copy of "Symbols of Peace" (handout #7) to each person.

+ Invite everyone to use the scrapbooking supplies on their tables to cut out the symbols for peace. They should write or draw something on at least two of the symbols that tells how they will bring peace to someone else.

+ After the groups have finished this part of the activity, invite each group member to set one symbol aside to place in the *We Believe & Celebrate First Penance* keepsake book or somewhere at home to serve as a reminder of our hope for peace. The remaining symbols at the table should be stapled together to form a peace chain.

+ Ask one person from each table group to bring the chain forward and use masking tape to attach it to two posters, creating a link between them. Realign the posters if the chains are not long enough.

Wrap-up *5 minutes*

+ Distribute copies of "Go in Peace" (handout #10) and the recipe for Vietnamese chicken salad (handout #1).

+ If time permits, elicit feedback from the group about this event. What have participants learned about the way Penance brings forgiveness, pardon, and peace?

Closing Prayer *10 minutes*

Draw the groups together and invite them to quiet themselves for prayer.

All stand.

Leader: God of mercy,
You sent your Son Jesus to show us how to love. We know that we do not always live in that love. For this we are sorry. In the Sacrament of Penance we ask for your forgiveness and pardon. Be with us now as we pray.

All: Amen.

All sit.

Invite the children who are preparing for First Penance to come forward. Gather them around the prayer table, facing the group. Refer to the heart medallions they are wearing, using these or similar words:

Leader: We have talked today about the different ways our hearts respond to God's call to let go of our sins and to accept the peace that comes from being forgiven and pardoned. You are preparing to celebrate the Sacrament of Penance for the first time.

Hold up the scrapbook page you created from handout #5.

Leader: I invite each of you to write your names on this heart. We will place it in our parish scrapbook and take it to Mass this week to remind the whole community to pray for you.

Each child signs the heart and then returns to his or her table group. Participants sing "Open Our Hearts." Explain that the posters displayed around the room represent the flow of the Sacrament of Penance. Invite all the participants to take a "heart walk," following the peace chain from one poster to the next. Ask the groups to bring their opening prayer sheets (handout #4) and to gather at the first poster. When the group has gathered, invite representative(s) to read the prayer(s) on their poster(s).

Leader: Let us walk the way of peace and live a life of love.

All: Amen.

Move as a group to the next poster, singing a verse of "Open Our Hearts." Follow the same prayer pattern at the remaining posters. Then, bring the entire group together to conclude the event in prayer.

Leader: Jesus teaches us to forgive, to accept God's pardon, and to walk the way of peace. May we open our hearts to receive God's love, given to us in the grace of the Holy Spirit. We ask this through Jesus, who is the heart of love and compassion.

All: Amen.

Leader: Our celebration is ended.
Let us go in peace.

All: Thanks be to God.

Song: "Take the Word of God with You"
(*We Believe & Celebrate First Penance/First Communion Music CD* #13)

Take the word of God with you as you go.
Take the seeds of God's word and make them grow.
Go in peace to serve the world in peace, to serve the world.
Take the love of God, the love of God with you as you go.

Go in peace to serve the world in peace, to serve the world.
Take the love of God, the love of God with you as you go.

33

After We Gather

(One day to two weeks after the event)

Follow-up is an important part of the *Gather In My Name* process. Here are some ideas for tying up loose ends and looking ahead to future events:

- ✦ If you did not use the evaluation form at the end of the event, send it to participants one to two weeks later. Completed forms will provide feedback about ways participants applied what was shared to their lives and will also help you in planning future events.

- ✦ Share your experience with the *Gather In My Name* writing team. As an individual or planning team, complete the feedback form and email it to webeditor@sadlier.com. If desired, send digital pictures of your event. We will email you a permissions form if we would like to use your photos on our web site.

- ✦ If you used the children's activity sheets during or after the event, you might want to set up a display where parishioners can view them. Do this one to two weeks after the event to help the rest of the parish learn about the sacramental preparation process.

- ✦ Place copies of "Go In Peace" (handout #10) with the bulletin or provide a link to it on the parish web site.

- ✦ Keep the parish keepsake scrapbook album in a visible place throughout the preparation process. Add pages by including copies of special bulletins, fliers, and prayer sheets along with short journaling pieces that explain what is going on.

- ✦ Display the heart page from the scrapbook with the children's signatures in a prominent place as a reminder to the community to pray for the children as they continue their preparation for the sacrament.

- ✦ Place copies of "Symbols of Peace" (handout #7) in a place where other members of the community can take one. Encourage them to complete the symbols and note how they will be agents of peace for others. **Option:** Use these symbols to extend the peace chain.

- ✦ Create a link to www.webelieveandcelebrate.com on your parish web site.

For your faith journey:

One of the first things I ever learned about Jesus was . . .

I remember Jesus . . .

Through receiving Jesus Christ in the Eucharist I . . .

We Believe & Celebrate First Communion

Components in this Section of the Guide

Getting Started (pages 35–36)
These pages will help you get organized. Here and at www.webelieveandcelebrate.com you will find all you need to begin as well as additional resources.

Two *Gather In My Name* Events (pages 37–62)
Developed as an alternative to the conventional parent meeting, these intergenerational sessions draw your entire parish community into the preparation process.

Event 1, "Memories of Jesus," helps households appreciate the power of memory in their lives, leading them to a deeper understanding of the Church's act of liturgical remembering (*anamnesis*).

Event 2, "Recognizing Jesus," sets the stage for recognizing the Real Presence of Jesus Christ in the Eucharist, which we receive as Holy Communion.

Participants at these two events will make a parish keepsake—a treasury of faith statements and prayers your parish community can cherish year after year.

ONLINE COMPONENTS
Visit www.webelieveandcelebrate.com

Setting the Schedule

All the elements of your sacramental preparation program hinge on the scheduling of the Mass during which the children will receive their first Holy Communion. Will they celebrate their First Communion at a specially scheduled Mass, or during the parish's regular Sunday Mass? Will you offer households more than one date for this celebration? What is the parish format? The size, resources, culture, and customs of your parish may dictate one format over another. Step back from all of these factors and consider: How will this celebration draw the children, their families, and the greater community into the sacramental life of the Church and lifelong love for the Eucharist? The chart below lists key strengths and challenges of each possible parish format.

Advance planning, preferably months in advance, is important. Start by establishing the date(s) for the children's First Communion. If you offer multiple celebrations over a number of Sundays, establish the first date, and work backwards from there to set dates for the rest of the program. Download a timetable at our web site.

Format	Strengths	Challenges
Specially Scheduled Mass One parish celebration, usually on a Saturday or Sunday, for First Communion candidates and their families	• Focused preparation • Children celebrate with peers who have prepared with them • Ability to select special liturgical options that enhance the celebration	• Less connection to the weekly parish Mass • Less involvement by the parish-at-large in the process and celebration
Sunday Mass Options **Groups** Two or more candidates and their families celebrate the sacrament during a regular Sunday liturgy **Individual Family** Each family selects a weekend to celebrate the child's first Holy Communion at the Sunday liturgy	• Connects directly to weekly celebration of the Eucharist: candidates celebrate the sacrament with people they see every Sunday • Renews appreciation of parish community for the sacrament • Emphasizes the role of the Catholic household in preparation and celebration	• Overcrowding or scheduling problems at Sunday liturgies • Adds time to the regular Sunday Mass, so parishioners must be informed before the celebrations

Getting Started

Involving Parents and Guardians

Parents and guardians play a primary role in the faith development of their children. *We Believe & Celebrate First Communion* promotes parental involvement through textbooks, lesson plans, and tools to help parents journey with their children toward the reception of their first Holy Communion.

Parent Letters

Parent Letter 1: *Welcome* gives an overview of the process, plus an invitation to the first *Gather In My Name* event. It includes a sample program schedule and a short article on discerning readiness for the sacrament throughout the preparation period.

Parent Letter 2: *Readiness* invites parents and guardians into the final preparation for the sacrament and reminds them of the second *Gather In My Name* event. If you will offer Readiness Meetings, this letter also provides that invitation.

There is also a parent letter for candidates who will receive the Sacraments of Initiation in the Proper Order (Confirmation and then Eucharist). Download this template at our web site.

Readiness Meeting for the Reception of First Holy Communion *(Optional)*

In the last few weeks before the celebration, you might want to schedule Readiness Meetings. Visit our web site for more information.

Involving Godparents

Help households understand Eucharist as a Sacrament of Initiation by including the child's godparents in the preparation process. Encourage parents to invite godparents to the *Gather In My Name* events. If time or distance prevents godparents from taking part, find other ways to involve them. Encourage candidates to interview godparents about the memories they have from the child's Baptism celebration. Send an eCard from our web site to godparents inviting them to stay in contact with the child throughout the preparation process. Invite families to bring their child's baptismal candle to the Eucharistic celebration. Provide extra candles in case a family forgets! During the Profession of Faith, have the children stand up front with their godparents, holding their lighted baptismal candles, as all recite the Creed.

The Praying Community

Many parishes invite members of the greater community to pray for and write notes to the children preparing to receive their first Holy Communion. This idea has been incorporated into the second *Gather In My Name* event for First Communion. Encourage parishioners to include a photograph of themselves with their note. This photograph will be a welcome addition to the child's keepsake book and will enable the child to easily recognize the parishioner in church or other places in the community.

First Communion Rehearsal

About a week before the Mass at which the children will receive their first Holy Communion, gather families for a rehearsal. This will prepare the children to receive the Body and Blood of Christ in Holy Communion reverently.

Remember that less is more. The more you give the children to rehearse or memorize, the less they will be able to focus on the spiritual dimension of the event. If you have special elements to rehearse or other announcements to make, save the practice of receiving the host as the last thing you do.

Be sure to explain that the bread and wine you are using is not the Body and Blood of Jesus because they have not been consecrated during the celebration of the Mass. Refer families to pages 79 and 80 of the keepsake book, "How to Receive Jesus in Holy Communion." Review the steps outlined in the book, and then invite the children to practice. As each child comes forward, take your time explaining the steps. Encourage all of the children to practice receiving from the chalice so that they will not be surprised by the taste.

When children come forward to receive the unconsecrated host, they will have questions about the taste of the host or the wine, or how to hold their hands or take the chalice. Walking through the procession, gestures, and reception of the host and chalice will ease anxieties and help parents to see aspects they can reinforce at home.

After all have practiced, remind everyone of the time after Holy Communion when they can offer a quiet prayer of thanks to Jesus. Lead a short prayer of intercession for all the children preparing to receive Jesus in Holy Communion. Joyfully remind the children that the next time they gather they will be able to receive Jesus in their first Holy Communion!

If children are preparing for Confirmation as part of the Proper Order of the Sacraments of Initiation, rehearse the Confirmation Rite. See page 64 of this guide for suggestions.

If you are planning to present the children with certificates after they celebrate the sacrament, complete them after the rehearsal. To order certificates, visit www.sadlier.com/catalog.

FIRST COMMUNION EVENT 1

Leader's Guide   Memories of Jesus

Objectives

To appreciate the importance of memories and how they are formed through the events, stories, people, and places that are part of our lives

To identify how our memories of Jesus were, and are, formed by our families, the liturgy and sacraments, and catechetical experiences

To learn the meaning of *anamnesis* as the liturgical act of remembering

To celebrate the way we are gathered in the name of Jesus and how he is present to us in our words, actions, and interrelationships

Faith Response

Participants will be able to name the ways they experience Jesus' presence through their memories as individuals, as families, and as a faith community.

Source Material

◆ Sadlier *We Believe & Celebrate First Communion*

◆ Sadlier Faith and Witness *Liturgy and Worship: A Course on Prayer and Sacraments*

◆ Schlabach, Joetta Handrich. *Extending the Table: A World Community Cookbook.* Pennsylvania: Herald Press, 1991.

◆ Bishops' Committee on the Liturgy. *Catholic Household Blessings and Prayers.* Washington, D.C.: United States Conference of Catholic Bishops, 1991.

Format Choice	GIMN Option 1	GIMN Option 2
What is it?	full multigenerational event	multigenerational event with breakout sessions
Who participates?	adults, children, and youth together for the entire session	adults, children, and youth come together for opening activities, then children break out into cluster groups
How do I follow this guide?	complete everything **except** the "Option 2 Only" tabs	complete everything **except** the "Option 1 Only" tabs for adults and youth; children's breakout session outlines online
What are the benefits?	the entire parish community partakes in the event together	expansive presentation for adults and older youth; age-appropriate presentation for First Communion, Confirmation, and Proper Order candidates

Background for Leaders and Adults

To memorize is to "learn by heart." We remember something because we have practiced it (a piece of music), we have repeated it (an exercise), or because it has become part of us. We share memories that have become part of our story—our journey of life. What we remember about Jesus comes to us from different sources: through reading and hearing the Gospel stories, through catechesis in our parish or school, and through what we hear from others, especially our families.

Anamnesis is the liturgical act of remembering. The celebration of the sacraments not only recalls the redemptive events of the past but also makes those events present and real to us today. Jesus' life, death, and Resurrection continue to be experienced by us in the present.

Option 1 Multigenerational Event

Option 2 Multigenerational Event with Breakout Sessions

Before We Gather

Publicity

Publicizing the event is an important component of preparation. Visit www.webelieveandcelebrate.com for resources.

Preparation

To prepare for this *Gather In My Name* (*GIMN*) event, you, the leader, are encouraged to read over all the material and familiarize yourself with the content and the process. The following guidelines will help you in preparing for the event. Download handouts and a preparation chart at our web site.

Preparing the Gathering Space

+ Set up enough tables that seat eight to ten people to accommodate your group.

+ Arrange childcare for children under the age of four.

Option 2 Only

+ Arrange space for breakout group meetings. Recruit catechists for each breakout group. Download outlines for the children's breakout sessions at our web site.

+ Set up a focal point for prayer. Spread a table with a decorative cloth of the appropriate liturgical color. Set up a Bible and a large candle.

+ On a side table, set a loaf of unsliced bread, a carafe of wine, and the scrapbook that will be used for the two First Communion *GIMN* events. If scrapbooks from past years are available, gather them as well.

✦ Set up one or two tables beside the prayer table to display completed scrapbook pages from the parish keepsake activity. Set up small boxes under seasonally appropriate cloths or small book stands to prop up the pages so that they are visible to participants.

✦ Make copies of the following handouts:
  • for each person: table blessing (handout #2); "Jesus, We Remember You" (handout #4); "Snapshots of Jesus" (handout #5)
  • for each household: recipe (handout #1); "Memories of Jesus" (handout #10)
  • for each table: "I Remember When" (handout #3); scrapbook page (handout #6); directions (handout #7). **Option:** In place of handout #6, purchase and use your own scrapbook paper.
  • for children and adults as needed: evaluation forms (handout #8); children's activity sheets (handout #9)

✦ Affix a piece of colored paper or card stock, large enough to mat a 4-by-6-inch photo, on each scrapbook page. Use scrapbooking techniques to title each page "Our memories of Jesus."

✦ Copy handout #11 and paste the picture on heavy cardstock. Cut out the puzzle pieces. Then trace the outline of each puzzle piece on a sheet of foam board so that the pieces are reconnected as a whole. Cut out the corresponding readings (handout #5) and set them aside. **Option:** Download a Power Point presentation at our web site in place of handout #11.

✦ Place the foam board on an easel by the prayer table. Set a glue stick nearby.

✦ Assemble a basket of scrapbooking supplies for each table. Each basket should include pens, pencils, markers, scissors, invisible tape, adhesive, and colored paper or tagboard. Include other embellishment items as desired, such as ribbon, string, glitter, or buttons.

✦ Recruit volunteers to photograph the table groups during the ice-breaker activity. If you will use a Polaroid camera, be sure to purchase enough film to take photos of each group. If you will use a digital or film camera, ask the photographer to devise a numbering system to match table group photos to their corresponding scrapbook pages.

✦ **Option:** Take two photos of each household, or make duplicate prints of the photos. Use one photo for the parish scrapbook page, and give or mail the other to each household.

✦ If you will distribute the *We Believe & Celebrate First Communion* keepsake books to the children preparing for First Communion, set these near the prayer table.

✦ **Option:** Obtain *First Communion* cross medallions (see www.sadlier.com/catalog to order).

Getting Started

After participants enter and register, invite them to be seated at one of the tables. Seat two to three households at each table, including those who are attending as individuals.

Ask four participants to be readers for the opening prayer. Give each one a puzzle piece (from handout #11) and the corresponding reading (handout #5). Demonstrate how and where to affix the puzzle pieces to their corresponding place on the foam board or the Power Point.

Ask three or more people to carry the loaf of bread, carafe of wine, and scrapbook(s) in the opening prayer procession.

If you will use the *We Believe & Celebrate First Penance/First Communion Music CD*, set up a CD player.

When We Gather

Meal Plan (Optional)

To build a greater sense of community, plan a festive meal before or after the event. Here are some ideas to consider as you plan:

✦ Invite the participants to create a memorable meal by bringing dishes that have a significance for their families. Ask households to share the story of their dish as part of the table conversation. Make batches of Kentucky cornbread (handout #1) and serve it with the meal.

✦ Plan an association meal by serving foods that represent different seasons and holidays of the year, such as pumpkin pie, Easter bread, and barbequed chicken. Invite participants to discuss the associations they make with each food.

✦ Recruit the families involved in First Communion preparation from the previous year to prepare, host, and serve the meal. Involve them in memory sharing as part of the first activity.

✦ Offer a table blessing (handout #2).

Opening/Ice-Breaker *10 minutes*

I Remember When

✦ Draw attention to "I Remember When" (handout #3). Explain the directions and invite the table groups to complete the activity.

✦ After about five minutes, invite a member of each group to share a memory with the larger group using one sentence, beginning with the phrase, "I remember when."

◆ Invite members of the large group to make observations about the memories various participants shared. Then continue the discussion at individual tables. Ask, "How did you feel while sharing the memories? What made the sharing striking or enjoyable?"

◆ As the groups talk, the photographer(s) should circulate from table to table taking pictures of households. If the group is large, the photographer could continue taking pictures during the opening prayer.

Session Overview *5 minutes*

◆ Introduce the session with the following points:

• Each of us has memories of special events, experiences, and people in our lives.

• As a Christian community, we have memories of Jesus and how he lived, died, and rose again. We celebrate these events each time we gather in his name.

• In this *Gather In My Name* event, we will talk about our personal memories of Jesus and the memories we hold as a community.

• This a memorable time in the life of our parish because many of you are beginning your preparation for First Communion.

◆ Ask the candidates for the sacrament to stand and invite the community to acknowledge them with applause. Remind them that the whole parish is praying for them as they prepare to receive Jesus. Acknowledge other groups at this time if appropriate.

◆ Add housekeeping and other announcements.

◆ The pastor might offer a brief word of welcome at this time.

◆ Distribute copies of "Jesus, We Remember You" (handout #4) and invite the groups to ready themselves for prayer.

Opening Prayer: Jesus, We Remember You *10 minutes*

The GIMN leader or the pastor serves as the leader of the opening prayer.

All stand.

Leader: Let us sing our opening song,
"We Remember You."
(*We Believe & Celebrate First Penance/First Communion Music CD #14*)

Jesus, we remember you.
Jesus, we remember you.
We remember you gave your life for us.
We remember. We believe.

We praise you, we remember you.
We bless you, we remember you,
And we thank you that we belong to you.
We remember. We believe.

During the opening hymn, the loaf of bread, carafe of wine, and scrapbook(s) are brought forward and placed on the prayer table.

Leader: We gather, as always, in the name of the Father,
and of the Son, and of the Holy Spirit.

All: Amen.

Leader: Let us pray.
God of salvation,
We remember Jesus.
We remember how he lived as one of us.
We remember how he gave his life for us.
We remember the gift that he gave to us when he said,
"Do this in memory of me."
We remember. We believe.
Open our hearts to your powerful presence
every time we remember him,
every time we do what he told us to do.
We ask this through the same Jesus Christ, your Son, who
lives and reigns with you and the Holy Spirit, one God,
forever and ever.

All: Amen.

All sit.

Leader: We shared memories today.

If the session began with a meal, say the following:

We shared a meal together. We talked and laughed and shared memories with one another.

As we gather now in prayer, we remember Jesus.
Let us respond to his story from the Gospel of Luke,
Chapter 22, with "Jesus, we remember you!"

Reader 1: "When the hour came, [Jesus] took his place at table with the apostles." (Luke 22:14)

All: Jesus, we remember you!

Reader 1 affixes the puzzle piece to the foam board or electronically using Power Point.

Reader 2: "He said to them, 'I have eagerly desired to eat this Passover with you before I suffer, for, I tell you, I shall not eat it [again] until there is fulfillment in the kingdom of God.'" (Luke 22:15–16)

All: Jesus, we remember you!

Reader 2 affixes the puzzle piece to the foam board or electronically using Power Point.

Reader 3: "He took the bread, said the blessing, broke it, and gave it to them, saying, 'This is my body, which will be given for you; do this in memory of me.'" (Luke 22:19)

All: Jesus, we remember you!

Reader 3 affixes the puzzle piece to the foam board or electronically using Power Point.

Reader 4: "And likewise the cup after they had eaten, saying, 'This cup is the new covenant in my blood, which will be shed for you.'" (Luke 22:20)

All: Jesus, we remember you!

Reader 4 affixes the puzzle piece to the foam board or electronically using Power Point.

All stand.

Leader: Let us pray.
We remember you, Lord Jesus,
and what you ask us to do.

All: Make our gathering holy;
make us one with you.

Leader: Thank you for memorable moments
that through life's journey we share,

All: especially the gift of the Eucharist,
and your living presence there.

Leader: We remember you, Lord Jesus,
let it be as Scripture said;

All: may we recognize and know you are there
in the Breaking of the Bread.
Amen!

Snapshots of Jesus *35 minutes*

Option 2 Only

Age Group Gatherings *5 minutes*

✦ After the opening prayer, divide the children into breakout groups with the catechists who will lead the breakout group sessions.

✦ After the children depart, invite the adults and remaining youth to form table groups of two to three households per table.

✦ Recall key elements of the ice-breaker and the opening prayer, using these or your own words:

- To memorize is to learn by heart. We remember something because we have practiced it, we have repeated it, or because it has become part of us.

- We shared memories that have become part of our story—our journey of life.

- What we remember about Jesus comes to us in different ways: through reading and hearing the Gospel stories, through catechesis in our parish or school, in the sacraments, and through what we hear from others, especially our families.

✦ Tell participants that they are going to explore their memories of Jesus.

Option 1 Only

✦ Invite participants to think about something they have learned about Jesus and how they learned it.

Option 2 Only

✦ Give participants an opportunity to reflect upon the following, using these or your own words:

- Take a few moments to reflect upon your journey of Catholic faith. For some of you, it began several years ago, as you were raised from childhood as a baptized member of the Church. For others, it began recently as you came into faith as an adult. Still others among you are beginning the journey as a disciple of Jesus now. Think about the very first experiences that brought you to faith, times when you met Jesus in an important way or learned something important about Jesus Christ.

- When did you first learn that Jesus was the Son of God? that Jesus suffered and died for us? that Jesus rose from the dead? that Jesus cared for the poor? that Jesus is the second Person of the Blessed Trinity? that Jesus is truly present in the Eucharist?

✦ Point out that these are foundational memories of Jesus. They are truths that parents and other adults help children to make part of their journey in faith.

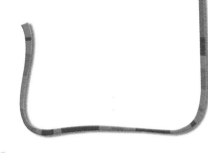

✦ Offer these or your own personal examples:

  • I remember that Jesus fed the hungry. When I was in first grade, my class put on a skit about the multiplication of the loaves. I played the child who brought bread and fish to Jesus who used them to feed five thousand people.

  • Jesus is my brother. When I went through the RCIA, I listened to the Gospel in a new way. Through talks with my sponsor, I began to connect the stories of Jesus to my own life.

✦ **Option:** Invite parents from last year's First Communion celebration or those who have gone through the RCIA to share their memories about Jesus.

✦ Note that one way to capture memories is by taking photos or snapshots. Briefly discuss that a snapshot is a picture that gives a quick impression or view of someone or something. We often collect these snapshots in albums or scrapbooks.

✦ Explain that each person is going to create a "snapshot" of Jesus that will be part of a very special parish scrapbook.

✦ Point out that the snapshot they will make is not a photograph, but rather an image of their memories of Jesus.

✦ Invite the participants at each table to talk about their memories of Jesus. Ask them to answer the following questions:

  • Recall a time when you learned something special or important about Jesus. What did you learn?

  • How did you learn it? Who helped you to learn it?

✦ Distribute a "Snapshot of Jesus" (handout #5) to each table.

✦ Allow ten minutes for the table groups to share their memories.

✦ Invite participants to make their own snapshots of Jesus. Have them cut apart the snapshot rectangles as directed and invite them to write or draw something that represents what they remember about Jesus. Ask everyone to write a phrase that describes what she or he has learned about Jesus on the lines provided.

✦ Invite participants to mount their snapshots on colored paper, leaving small borders around them.

✦ While the groups are making their snapshots, circulate from table to table to answer questions and provide additional assistance. If experienced scrapbookers are available, have them circulate to offer assistance.

Option 1 Only

✦ As participants complete the activity, invite them to take a break.

Break *10 minutes*

Making a Parish Keepsake *20 minutes*

✦ Introduce the activity with these or similar words:

- Each of us has had time to assemble our own snapshot of Jesus. This marks a time when you met Jesus in a significant way or learned something important about him.

- A scrapbook is a keepsake, one that preserves memorable moments in our lives.

- This is a memorable time in the life of our parish family as we celebrate with those who are preparing for First Communion (and full initiation or Confirmation).

- By compiling our snapshots in a scrapbook, we can show the ways we are living the Good News of Jesus. We show how we not only remember what Jesus did so many years ago, but also the ways he is present and real to us today.

✦ Distribute a copy of the scrapbook pages and directions (handouts #6 and #7) to each table.

✦ Invite the table groups to affix their snapshots to their pages and add embellishments as desired. If photos of the groups are available, distribute them and have groups mount them on the mat space.

✦ Distribute copies of the evaluation (handout #8) and children's activity sheet (handout #9). As groups finish the activity, invite them to complete the evaluation forms.

Wrap-up *5 minutes*

✦ Distribute copies of "Memories of Jesus" (handout #10) and the recipe for Kentucky cornbread (handout #1).

✦ If time permits, elicit feedback from the group about this event. Ask participants what they have learned about Jesus and how this event and faith sharing have enriched their memories of Jesus.

Option 2 Only

✦ Allow ten to fifteen minutes for each table to complete their snapshots.

✦ Distribute copies of "Memories of Jesus" (handout #10).

✦ Allow tables five minutes to discuss the following questions. For ease of discussion, post the questions on a white board or flip chart.

- As you shared your memories of Jesus, what similarities did you notice, either in the memories themselves or how you learned about Jesus?

- What differences did you notice?

- What did this sharing of memories tell you about the power of memories?

✦ Wrap up this activity with the following points:

- Memories have power. When we share our personal memories, we reexperience them and keep them alive. Shared memories and stories are part of the glue that keeps households and families together.

- Your snapshot of Jesus is an important part of your story of faith. Sharing these memories of Jesus is part of the glue that keeps our family of faith, the Church, together.

- In just a few moments, we will assemble all of our snapshots into a parish keepsake. As we do this, reflect upon the power of our shared memory.

- As our candidates prepare to receive Jesus for the first time in Holy Communion, they need all of us to share these important stories of Jesus with them.

✦ Refer to the definition of anamnesis on "Memories of Jesus" (handout #10). Emphasize that it is the Church's liturgical act of remembering and that it not only entails remembering events of the past but also makes Jesus present to us here and now through the sacraments.

✦ Invite the participants to take a break. After the break, ask them to return to the table at which they started the event.

✦ As the children return from the breakout groups, help them find their household groups.

Closing Prayer *10 minutes*

Draw the groups together and invite them to quiet themselves for prayer. Ask them to look at their scrapbook page and to reflect on the following questions: What do you see in the memories of Jesus? How do you feel as you see all of the snapshots together on the page?

Leader: It is exciting to see our memories of Jesus together.
Let's take a moment to admire them.

Invite someone from each table to hold up their group's scrapbook page for all participants to admire.

Leader: We started our event with our individual snapshots,
our personal memories of Jesus.
Bringing them together makes our memories even
more powerful.
When we gather together as a Christian community,
we celebrate what we remember about Jesus and
we thank God for his presence with us now.
Let us thank God for the gift of faith that we share.

All stand.

Leader: Loving God,
We thank you for gathering us together in the
name of your Son, Jesus.
We thank you for the memories we have and for
all those who have helped us learn about Jesus.
When we remember, we know that Jesus is with us today.
Help us to grow in our love of Jesus.
We pray this in his holy name through the power of
the Holy Spirit.

All: Amen.

Invite a representative from each table to come forward with the scrapbook page and to prop it on the table in the prayer space while the entire group sings "We Remember You."

After all the pages have been brought forward, point out that they will be assembled in a single book and included in prayers and blessings throughout the sacramental preparation process.

Invite the children preparing for First Communion (or full initiation and Confirmation) to stand with their parents and guardians.

As you offer the following prayer, invite the parents to sign their children on the ears and mouth.

Leader: Dear children,
In baptism you were claimed for Christ.
May God bless you now and watch over you.
May the Lord Jesus touch your ears to receive his word,
and your mouth to proclaim his faith.
May you come with joy to his supper
to the praise and glory of God.

All: Amen.
(Adapted from *Catholic Household Blessings and Prayers*)

If you are distributing the We Believe & Celebrate First Communion *keepsake books and crosses at this time, invite the children to come forward to receive them. Afterwards, ask the entire community to acknowledge the children with a round of applause.*

Leader: Our celebration is over.
Let us go forth to love and serve the Lord.

All: Thanks be to God.

Song: "We Remember You"

After We Gather

(One day to two weeks after the event)

Follow-up is an important part of the *Gather In My Name* process. Here are some ideas for tying up loose ends and looking ahead to future events:

- ✦ If you did not use the evaluation form at the end of the event, send it to participants one to two weeks later. Completed forms will provide feedback about ways participants applied what was shared to their lives and will also help you in planning future events.

- ✦ Share your experience with the *Gather In My Name* writing team. As an individual or planning team, complete the feedback form and email it to webeditor@sadlier.com. If desired, send digital pictures of your event. We will email you a permissions form if we would like to use your photos on our web site.

- ✦ If you used the children's activity sheets during or after the event, you might want to set up a display where parishioners can view them. Do this one to two weeks after the event to help the rest of the parish learn about the sacramental preparation process.

- ✦ Place copies of "Memories of Jesus" (handout #10) with the bulletin or provide a link to it on the parish web site.

- ✦ Keep the parish keepsake scrapbook album in a visible place throughout the preparation process. Add pages by including copies of special bulletins, fliers, and prayer sheets along with short journaling pieces that explain what is going on. Take pictures of the children and their families as they gather for catechetical sessions and parish liturgies and make a page about each one.

- ✦ Create a link to www.webelieveandcelebrate.com on your parish web site. Invite the children who attended the *GIMN* event to send an eCard from this site to thank someone for helping them remember Jesus.

- ✦ If you will mail photos to households after the event, invite those preparing for First Communion to use them for the scrapbooking activity on page 17 of their *We Believe & Celebrate First Communion* keepsake book.

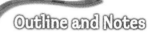

FIRST COMMUNION EVENT 2

Leader's Guide Recognizing Jesus

Objectives

To learn how the four parts of the Emmaus story (Luke 24:13–35) can help us to understand the Mass and open us to ways of recognizing Christ in our midst

To understand the Eucharist as a communal action and to appreciate how it celebrates the abiding presence of Jesus among us

To identify ways that we can recognize Jesus when we choose to treat one another with love, respect, generosity, hospitality, and caring

To provide an opportunity for the parish community to support and encourage the candidates for First Communion

Faith Response

Participants will be able to name the ways we recognize the Real Presence of Jesus in the celebration of the Eucharist and in the ways we share his love with others.

Source Material

✦ Sadlier *We Believe & Celebrate First Penance*

✦ Sadlier Faith and Witness *Liturgy and Worship: A Course on Prayer and Sacraments*

✦ Schlabach, Joetta Handrich. *Extending the Table: A World Community Cookbook.* Pennsylvania: Herald Press, 1991.

Format

Gather In My Name is a full multigenerational event of approximately ninety minutes with the optional inclusion of a meal.

Outline and Notes

Background for Leaders and Adults

When we celebrate the Eucharist, we gather to experience the Real Presence of Christ in our midst. This is an active process and communal action, one that requires the participation of each member of the Body of Christ. The account of the disciples on the road to Emmaus (Luke 24:13–35) provides a framework for understanding the fourfold structure of the Mass:

◆ We gather.

◆ We listen to the stories (readings) of our faith.

◆ We prepare our gifts, celebrate the Eucharistic Prayer, and share Communion.

◆ We go forth to share the Good News of Jesus with others.

As children continue their initiation into the Church through the celebration of First Communion, they are invited to participate more fully in this work of the Christian community—the liturgy. They are accompanied by their families, friends, peers, and the faith community who help them recognize Jesus within the Eucharist and in the daily interactions and special moments that make up their lives.

Before We Gather

Publicity

Publicizing the event is an important component of preparation. Visit www.webelieveandcelebrate.com for resources.

Preparation

To prepare for this event, you, the leader, are encouraged to read over all the material and familiarize yourself with the content and the process. The following guidelines will help you in preparing for the event. Download handouts and a preparation chart at our web site.

Preparing the Gathering Space

◆ Set up enough tables that seat eight to ten people to accommodate your group.

◆ Arrange childcare for children under the age of four.

◆ Set up a focal point for prayer. Spread a table with a decorative cloth of the appropriate liturgical color. Set up a Bible and a large candle.

◆ Set up one or two tables beside the prayer table to display completed scrapbook pages. Set up small boxes under seasonally appropriate cloths or small book stands to prop up the pages so that they are visible to participants.

◆ On a side table, set a loaf of unsliced bread, a carafe of wine, and the scrapbook that was created in the "Memories of Jesus" *GIMN* event. If scrapbooks from the past year are available, gather them as well.

- ◆ Make copies of the following handouts:
  - for each person: table blessing (handout #2), "When I Think of . . . " (handout #3); "Their Eyes Were Opened" (handout #4)
  - for each household: recipe (handout #1); "Recognizing Jesus" (handout #10)
  - for each table: a scrapbook page (handout #6); directions (handout #7). Use scrapbooking techniques to title each scrapbook page "We help others recognize Jesus."
  - for children and adults as needed: children's activity sheets (handout #9); evaluation forms (handout #8)
- ◆ Read over the opening prayer.
- ◆ If you will use the *We Believe & Celebrate First Penance/First Communion Music CD*, set up a CD player.
- ◆ Use signs to number tables from one to four. If there are more than four tables, place duplicate numbers on extra tables.
- ◆ Copy "Glimpses of Jesus" (handout #5) so that each table receives a different page: #5A, #5B, #5C, or #5D. If there are more than four tables, assign the same page to multiple tables.
- ◆ Assemble a basket of scrapbooking supplies for each table. Include pens, pencils, markers, scissors, invisible tape, adhesive, and colored paper or tagboard. Include other embellishment items as desired, such as ribbon, string, glitter, or buttons.
- ◆ Invite three or four representatives from the parish community to attend and serve as witnesses during the closing prayer. Choose people who represent different aspects of your parish, such as a pastoral council member, a teenager or Confirmation candidate, a family member who celebrated First Communion the previous year, a priest, an extraordinary minister of the Eucharist, or a homebound parishioner. (Ask for a statement from the homebound parishioner if that parishioner is unable to attend.)
- ◆ Explain that these representatives will offer, in three or four sentences, a personal testimonial of how they recognize Jesus in the Eucharist, opening with the statement "I recognize Jesus when . . . ."
- ◆ Instruct witnesses that these testimonials are short, personal stories that recount how they feel and how they are inspired. Provide the following example: "I recognize Jesus when I come forward for Communion. When the Eucharistic minister says 'The Body of Christ,' and looks at me with caring, I know that Jesus is there, and that his Body and Blood will strengthen me. What an awesome gift!"
- ◆ Arrange for parishioners to write a letter to each child preparing for First Communion. Make sure you have a letter for every child. **Option:** Ask the parishioner to enclose a photo so that the child can recognize the parishioner at Mass. Place these letters in a basket near the prayer table.

Getting Started

After participants enter and register, invite them to be seated at one of the tables. Seat two to three households at each table, including those who are attending as individuals.

Ask three people to carry the loaf of bread, the carafe of wine, and scrapbook in the opening prayer procession.

Recruit three volunteers to act out the Emmaus story as the table groups read it during the opening prayer. Provide ideas for each scene as needed.

When We Gather

Meal Plan *(Optional)*

To build a greater sense of community, plan a festive meal before or after the event. Here are some ideas to consider as you plan:

✦ Invite the participants to break bread. Make a large batch of chicken salad (handout #1) and invite each household to bring bread or rolls.

✦ Ask different parish groups to sponsor a meal for the event as a way to show love and support for the First Communion candidates and their families.

✦ Offer a table blessing (handout #2).

Opening/Ice-Breaker *10 minutes*

✦ Draw attention to "When I Think Of . . ." (handout #3). Read the directions together and invite the table groups to complete the activity.

✦ After the groups have completed the activity, draw them back together. Ask groups to share their responses to the last question: "What makes you think of Jesus?"

Session Overview *5 minutes*

✦ Introduce the session with the following points:

• Certain things and actions make us think of particular times, people, and events in our lives.

• As a Christian community, we come together each week for the Eucharist. The words we say and things we do celebrate the presence of Jesus among us.

• In this *Gather In My Name* event, we will talk about ways we recognize the presence of Jesus in the Eucharist. We will also name ways we can help others recognize Jesus in the things we do to show our love.

• Some members of our parish are here to share stories about the ways they recognize Jesus through the ministries they carry out.

✦ Invite this group to stand and welcome them.

- ✦ Ask the First Communion candidates and candidates for the Sacraments of Initiation to stand. Note what a special time this is for them. Explain that, as their families, friends, and members of their parish, we want to help them recognize Jesus through the celebration of the sacraments and in their daily lives.

- ✦ Add housekeeping and other announcements.

- ✦ The pastor might offer a brief word of welcome at this time.

- ✦ Distribute copies of "Their Eyes Were Opened" (handout #4) and invite the groups to ready themselves for prayer.

- ✦ **Option:** Present each candidate with their own copy of *With Jesus Always*. For ordering information, visit www.sadlier.com/catalog.

Opening Prayer: **Their Eyes Were Opened** *10 minutes*

The GIMN leader or the pastor serves as the leader of the opening prayer.

All stand.

Leader: Let us sing our opening song,
"Jesus, You Are Bread for Us."
(*We Believe & Celebrate First Penance/First Communion Music CD #15*)

All: Jesus, you are bread for us.
Jesus, you are life for us.
In your gift of Eucharist, we find love.
When we feel we need a friend, you are there with us, Jesus.
Thank you for the friend you are.
Thank you for the love we share.

*During the opening hymn, the loaf of bread, carafe of wine, and
scrapbook(s) are brought forward and placed on the prayer table.*

Leader: Let us begin our prayer as we do each time
we gather for the Eucharist.
In the name of the Father, and of the Son,
and of the Holy Spirit.

All: Amen.

All sit.

Leader: In our opening activity, we shared how certain
words, foods, songs, actions, sights, sounds, and
smells remind us of special times or experiences.
We will listen to a story about two disciples who did
not recognize the risen Jesus although he was walking and
talking with them. Their eyes were finally opened when he
did something special with them.

*Invite the volunteers who will act out the story to come forward. Invite the tables to read
aloud the part of the story on their prayer sheet that corresponds with their table number.*

Leader: The following is a reading adapted from the holy Gospel
according to Luke.

All: Glory to you, Lord.

Table 1:   It was the Sunday that Jesus had risen from the dead. Two of
Jesus' disciples were walking to Emmaus, a town near Jerusalem.

Table 2:   A man met the disciples on the road. He started walking with
them. They did not know that this man was the risen Jesus.

Table 3:   The disciples told him that they were talking about the past three
days. Jesus was crucified, died, and was buried. And now his body
was missing from the tomb.

Table 4: It was getting dark when they reached the town. The disciples asked the man to stay with them. He did stay. "While he was with them at table, he took bread, said the blessing, broke it, and gave it to them." (Luke 24:30)

Leader: Then the disciples recognized that this man was the risen Jesus! They knew him "in the breaking of the bread" (Luke 24:35).

The Gospel of the Lord.

All: Praise to you, Lord Jesus Christ.

Leader: Let us pray.

All stand.

Leader: Lord Jesus,
be with us as we gather in your name.
Open our eyes so that we may see you
in the ordinary events of our lives.
Give us a greater appreciation for the gift
of the Eucharist and for one another.
Help us to grow in love and show us
how to share that love with all we meet.

In your holy name we pray.

All: Amen!

Glimpses of Jesus *30 minutes*

✦ Recall the Gospel story read in the opening prayer. Ask these or similar questions and draw out the responses that follow:

• Why didn't the disciples recognize Jesus when he joined them on the road? (They thought he was dead.)

• What did the disciples tell Jesus? (They told him the story of how Jesus was crucified, died, and was buried, and how his body was missing from the tomb.)

• What finally caused the disciples to recognize Jesus? (He blessed the bread, broke it, and gave it to them.)

• Why did this cause the disciples' eyes to be opened? (They had seen Jesus do this before; it was a special ritual they shared with the rest of their community.)

✦ Point out that, like the disciples, we need to have "open eyes" to recognize how Jesus is present to us in the people, things, and experiences of our daily lives. Emphasize that the Eucharist celebrates Jesus in our midst.

✦ Explain that the participants will design some other scenes like the Emmaus story, in which we have opportunities to glimpse Jesus in the ordinary events of our lives.

✦ Distribute "Glimpses of Jesus" (handout #5), giving each group the scenario that corresponds with the number on their table: scenario 1, scenario 2, scenario 3, or scenario 4.

✦ Invite the table groups to read about their scenarios and to write a brief skit that illustrates how they might glimpse Jesus in a simple action or ritual. Everyone should have a part to play in the skit.

✦ Ask participants to complete the unfinished sentence at the bottom of the page with a word or phrase when they have finished planning their skit. Designate someone to read it during the closing prayer.

✦ Allow ten minutes for the groups to prepare their skits. Be available to answer questions and provide guidance.

✦ When all groups are ready, ask everyone to be seated. Call the first group(s) forward to present their skit(s) for scenario 1. After the scenario(s), ask the large group: "What glimpse of Jesus did you see in the scene(s)?"

✦ Proceed in the same manner with the other three scenarios. After each one, ask the same question and elicit responses from the large group.

✦ Acknowledge the creativity of all the table groups by leading a round of applause.

✦ In these or your own words, make the following points:

• Each time we celebrate the Eucharist we do so in a way that reflects the Emmaus story and the skits we presented.

- We gather together and welcome one another, especially those whom we do not know. We celebrate the Eucharist as a community of believers where all are welcome in the name of Jesus.

- We listen to stories of our faith in the readings from the Bible. Just as families pass on their special stories, we tell and retell our stories of faith. Jesus is present to us in God's Word. After the Gospel, we show our recognition of Jesus when we respond, "Praise to you, Lord Jesus Christ."

- We prepare our gifts, pray the Eucharistic Prayer, and share the Body and Blood of Christ in Communion. The words and actions that we use over and over again form a ritual that helps us recognize Jesus in our midst.

- We go forth to "love and serve the Lord." We take the Good News about Jesus and share it in the ways we show our love to others. We recognize Jesus in the world and help others to see him in the things we say and do.

◆ Explain that, after a break, we will discuss ways to help others recognize Jesus.

Break *10 minutes*

Making A Parish Keepsake *30 minutes*

◆ Introduce the activity with these or similar words:

- In your skits, people came to recognize Jesus in the midst of everyday life.

- In the original Emmaus story, what did the disciples do when they recognized Jesus? (They were excited and immediately went to tell the others they had seen Jesus.)

- Think back on the ways that we recognize Jesus. How can we help others to recognize Jesus? What can we say? What can we do?

◆ Distribute a scrapbook page and a set of directions (handouts #6 and #7) to each table.

◆ Inform participants that they will make another keepsake page for the parish scrapbook to show how their households help others to recognize Jesus.

◆ If experienced scrapbookers are available, have them circulate and offer ideas.

Wrap-up *5 minutes*

◆ Distribute copies of "Recognizing Jesus" (handout #10) and the recipe for chicken salad (handout #1).

◆ If time permits, elicit feedback from the group about this event. How have participants learned to recognize Jesus in the people and experiences of their lives?

Closing Prayer *10 minutes*

Invite participants to quiet themselves for prayer. Ask them to look at their scrapbook pages and to reflect on the following questions: What do you see in the ways we help others to recognize Jesus? Take a moment to admire the pages of tables around you. What do you notice? How do you feel? If time allows, invite short responses from the group.

Leader: Today we shared ways that we recognize Jesus and help others to recognize him. In our Scripture story we heard how Jesus' closest friends came to recognize him.

Quote the Scripture from Chapter 5 of the We Believe & Celebrate First Communion *keepsake book: Then the disciples recognized that this man was the risen Jesus! They knew him "in the breaking of the bread" (Luke 24:35).*

Leader: When the risen Jesus broke bread with his friends, they instantly knew who he was. This story reminds us of the wonderful way we come to know and recognize Jesus: in the celebration of the Eucharist. With gratitude, let us pray.

All stand.

Leader: Powerful God,
we thank you, we praise you, and we bless you.
You are with us every time we gather for Mass,
and your Son and Holy Spirit fill us with grace.
We thank you for the way we meet Jesus in your word.
We praise you for his presence in our brothers and sisters,
who worship with us.
We bless you for the way we see Jesus in the words, prayers,
and actions of the priest.
We thank you, we praise you, we bless you, God,
as we recognize Jesus in the consecrated bread and wine,
which become the Body and Blood of Christ for us.
Thank you, God, for helping us to recognize Jesus
in the gift of the Eucharist.
We pray this in his holy name by the power of the Holy Spirit.

All: Amen.

Leader:

Song: "Jesus, You Are Bread for Us"
(*We Believe & Celebrate First Penance/First Communion Music CD* #15)

All: Jesus, you are bread for us.
Jesus, you are life for us.
In your gift of Eucharist, we find love.
When we feel we need a friend, you are there with us, Jesus.
Thank you for the friend you are.
Thank you for the love we share.

All Sit.

After the refrain, an instrumental version of the hymn continues quietly as the representatives from the parish community come forward to witness to how they recognize Jesus in the Eucharist. After each witness finishes his or her statement, the large group responds by singing the refrain of the song. Invite a representative from each table to bring their keepsake page forward and place it on the table in the prayer space. As they do so, they offer the prayer from their group.

Leader:　Dear friends, as we give thanks for the ways that our brothers and sisters recognize Jesus in the Eucharist, we ask God to be with those who will receive Jesus for the very first time.

Invite those who will celebrate First Communion to stand with their parents and inform the children that members of the parish have written letters to them to offer their love and support during this time of preparation. If the group of children is large, ask for help from parents or older siblings to help distribute a letter to each child. Invite the children to place these letters in their keepsake books when they return home. If distributing With Jesus Always, *do so now. Ask everyone to stand and to raise their hands in blessing over the children as you pray.*

Leader:　Heavenly Father,
as these children prepare to
receive the Eucharist for the first time,
fill them with joy and excitement.
Help them to know in their hearts
the saving love of Jesus, your Son.
He was born for us,
walked among us,
and suffered and died for us.
He rose again in glory,
ascended into heaven,
and is with us every time we eat his Body and drink his Blood.

Father, make us all one,
so that, one day,
we may all share in eternal life with you.

We ask this through Jesus, who is bread for us, and the Spirit who gives us life, in union with you, forever and ever!

All:　Amen.

Leader:　Our celebration is ended.
Let us go forth to love and serve the Lord.

All:　Thanks be to God.

Invite participants to sing one of the parish's favorite hymns of praise before you conclude.

After We Gather

(One day to two weeks after the event)

Follow-up is an important part of the *Gather In My Name* process. Here are some ideas for tying up loose ends and looking ahead to future events:

✦ If you did not use the evaluation form at the end of the event, you might want to send it to participants one to two weeks later. Completed forms will provide feedback about ways in which participants applied what was shared to their lives and will help you in planning future events.

✦ Share your experience with the *Gather In My Name* writing team. As an individual or planning team, complete the feedback form and email it to webeditor@sadlier.com. If desired, send digital pictures of your event. We will email you a permissions form if we would like to use your photos on our web site.

✦ If you used the children's activity sheets during or after the event, you might want to set up a display where parishioners can view them. Do this one to two weeks after the event to help the rest of the parish learn about the sacramental preparation process.

✦ Place copies of "Recognizing Jesus" (handout #10) with the bulletin or provide a link to it on the parish web site.

✦ Keep the parish keepsake scrapbook album in a visible place throughout the preparation process. Add pages by including copies of special bulletins, fliers, and prayer sheets along with short journaling pieces that explain what it going on.

✦ Create a link to www.webelieveandcelebrate.com on your parish web site. Invite the children who attended the *Gather In My Name* event to send an eCard from this site to someone they would like to thank for helping them to recognize Jesus.

We Believe & Celebrate Proper Order

Components in this Section of the Guide

Getting Started (pages 63–64)
The following section provides assistance for parishes celebrating the Sacraments of Initiation in their proper order, with Confirmation taking place after Baptism and before First Communion. If you are unfamiliar with the process, or the rationale for celebrating Confirmation before First Communion, be sure to read the article entitled "Frequently Asked Questions about Confirmation in the Proper Order" that accompanies Parent Letter 1 at www.webelieveandcelebrate.com.

If your parish is celebrating the Sacrament of Confirmation in the Proper Order for the first time, parents will need to understand the parish decision. They may also express concern that Confirmation will be eclipsed by the celebration of First Communion. Be patient with these concerns, but emphasize that this combined celebration is not new. It is not only a return to the ancient practices of our Church, it is also part of our recent history. Children and adults who become Catholic through the Rite of Christian Initiation of Adults (RCIA) have been receiving Baptism, Confirmation, and Eucharist at the same liturgy for years.

The Proper Order Guide and Lesson (pages 65–73)
This section includes a guide and Lesson 3A: "We Receive the Sacrament of Confirmation." Your catechists or parents should use this lesson after Chapter 3: "We Celebrate the Liturgy of the Word" in the *We Believe & Celebrate First Communion* keepsake book. You may copy the lesson pages for each child. Since this is the only lesson for the Sacrament of Confirmation, you might want to schedule it as a special parish-based session and invite parents or guardians to attend. Include time at the end of the lesson to answer questions about the sacrament.

Getting Started

Involving Parents and Guardians

Parent Letters
Owners of this manual may download parent letter templates from www.webelieveandcelebrate.com and customize them to include specific program information. There are two letters for Proper Order:

Parent Letter 1: *Welcome* gives an overview of the process and an invitation to the first *Gather In My Name* event. It includes a program schedule template, plus two articles: "Frequently Asked Questions about Confirmation in the Proper Order" and "Is My Child Ready for Confirmation and First Communion?"

Parent Letter 2: *Readiness* invites parents and guardians into the final preparation for the sacraments and reminds them of the second *Gather In My Name* event. If you choose to offer Readiness Meetings, this letter also provides that invitation.

Readiness Meeting for Confirmation and First Communion *(Optional)*
A Readiness Meeting is a helpful way to work with parents to determine a child's preparedness for the celebration of the two sacraments. The Readiness Meeting is also a good opportunity to review the Rite of Confirmation with children and to discuss their responses about the gifts of the Holy Spirit on the scrapbook pages at the end of Lesson 3A. Visit our web site for more information.

The Confirmation Sponsor
Each candidate for Confirmation will need a sponsor. This should be a person who will be a spiritual guide for the child to help the child live as a true witness to Christ. It is desirable that baptismal godparents also serve as the child's sponsor (*Code of Canon Law*, Canon 893, §2). In fact, it is allowable to have two sponsors, especially if these are the child's godparents. This helps the child make the connection between Baptism and Confirmation.

Parent Letter 1 encourages parents and guardians to invite sponsors to the *Gather In My Name* events. Consider other ways to draw sponsors into the process. The *Involving Godparents* section on page 36 of this guide offers additional suggestions.

The Celebration Liturgy
While other strategies are possible, this guide assumes that you will celebrate Confirmation at the same liturgy in which you celebrate First Communion. Doing so accomplishes three things:

1. It helps parishioners understand that Eucharist completes our initiation into the Church.

2. It echoes the practice of the early Church, when the Sacraments of Baptism, Confirmation, and the Eucharist were celebrated all at once.

3. It follows the same pattern that is used for the initiation of Catholics through the RCIA.

If your diocese calls for the celebration of Confirmation at another liturgy, adapt the program schedule accordingly. Download the Rite of Confirmation at our web site.

The Rehearsal
There is a full description of a First Communion rehearsal on page 36 of this guide. When preparing to celebrate both Confirmation and First Communion, allow extra time for the rehearsal. If possible, invite sponsors to participate in the rehearsal. Since Confirmation takes place first in the liturgy, practice it first.

Well before the rehearsal, read through the Rite of Confirmation and think through seating plans, roles, and actions of candidates and sponsors during each part of the rite: the Presentation of the Candidates, the Homily, the Renewal of Baptismal Promises, the Laying on of Hands, and the Anointing with Chrism. Make notes of what they need to do when. Remember to keep it simple! Recruit and train assistants to usher candidates forward at the proper times during the Mass.

Walk the children and sponsors through the parts of the rite that demand their active response: the Renewal of Baptismal Promises and the Anointing with Chrism, with stand-ins taking the place of the bishop or priest.

Guide for Proper Order: Optional Lesson 3A
We Receive the Sacrament of Confirmation

STEP 1

We Gather *(pages 66–67)*

Discuss times when families give and receive gifts. You might have the children think about things in their homes that were gifts from someone. Ask, "Why do we give gifts?"

Invite the children to think about gifts they have received. Ask, "What are some special gifts you have received?"

Help the children draw or use scrapbooking materials to complete the first line, "One of the best gifts I have received is. . . ."

Ask, "What are some gifts you have given to other people?" Invite children to use words, drawing, or scrapbooking to complete the second line, "One of the best gifts that I ever gave was. . . . " Allow sharing if time permits.

We Share God's Word *(page 68)*

Invite volunteers to read the story aloud. Explain that this story comes from the Bible, the written word of God. It tells the story of Pentecost, the day that the Holy Spirit came to the disciples. You might write the word *Pentecost* on the board.

Ask, "What special gift did Jesus' disciples receive? What did the disciples do after they received the Holy Spirit?"

Direct attention to the Scripture art. Ask, "What do you see happening in the picture?" Highlight that the disciples are sharing the Good News. Explain that the Holy Spirit helped the disciples to do this. The Holy Spirit brought them courage. Ask, "What gift did the disciples give to the other people?" (the Good News of Jesus)

STEP 2

We Believe and Celebrate *(pages 69–70)*

Read aloud the first three paragraphs. Stress that we receive the Gift of the Holy Spirit in Confirmation. Ask, "Why did the Father and Jesus send the Holy Spirit?" (to help and guide the Church) "What does the Holy Spirit help us to do?" (to be followers of Jesus)

Emphasize that this is a special time of preparation for the Sacrament of Confirmation. We receive Confirmation only once.

Read aloud the remaining paragraphs on page 69 and first two paragraphs on page 70. Invite the children to think about the names and sponsors they will choose. Encourage them to talk with their parents about the choices they have to make.

We Believe and Celebrate *(pages 70–71)*

Introduce the third paragraph on page 70 by saying, "Here is what happens at the celebration of Confirmation." Read the rest of pages 70–71 aloud.

Stress the essential rite of Confirmation which is the laying on of the bishop's hands while anointing with blessed oil and the words, "N., be sealed with the Gift of the Holy Spirit." Have the children highlight or underline these sections on the page.

Remind the children that Confirmation leads to the Eucharist. In Holy Communion they will receive the Body and Blood of Jesus.

STEP 3

We Respond *(page 72)*

Read aloud the first paragraph on page 72. Help the children to read the gifts and how they will help us.

Discuss the ways the children think each gift will help them in their lives. Invite each child to name one gift of the Holy Spirit he or she will use.

Encourage the children to complete the sentences by writing, drawing, or scrapbooking.

We Respond in Prayer *(page 73)*

Prepare to pray. You will need a red cloth, a container with perfumed oil, and a small bowl of water. Play "We Believe, We Believe in God," #11 on the *We Believe & Celebrate CD.*

Read aloud the opening introduction of the prayer.

Pray the Sign of the Cross together. Pray the Leader parts and ask the children to pray the responses. Sing the song together.

Proper Order: Optional Lesson 3A

We Receive the Sacrament of Confirmation

One of the best gifts that I have received is ...

"Be sealed with the Gift of the Holy Spirit."

Rite of Confirmation

One of the best gifts that I ever gave was ...

We Share God's Word

📖 Acts of the Apostles 2:1–4, 38

One of the gifts that Jesus promised to send to his followers is God the Holy Spirit. And Jesus kept his promise. After Jesus Christ suffered, died, and rose again, here is what happened:

Reader 1: The Apostles and Mary and some of Jesus' disciples were gathered in one place together.

Reader 2: Suddenly they heard a loud noise, like a strong wind blowing.

Reader 3: And then flames appeared over each person's head, "and they were all filled with the holy Spirit" (Acts of the Apostles 2:4).

Reader 4: They went out and started to tell others the Good News of God's love.

We Believe and Celebrate

The Holy Spirit is God, the third Person of the Blessed Trinity. The Holy Spirit was sent by the Father and Jesus to help and guide the Church. The Holy Spirit helps us to be strong followers of Jesus. We show that we follow Jesus by the way we live.

The Holy Spirit is still with us today. We celebrate the Gift of the Holy Spirit in the Sacrament of Confirmation.

Preparing for the Sacrament of Confirmation is an important time for us. We pray and learn more about the Holy Spirit. At Confirmation we choose a name of a saint whose example we can follow in growing closer to Jesus. Taking the same name given to us at Baptism shows the close connection between Baptism and Confirmation.

In Baptism, each of us received the Holy Spirit. We became children of God and members of the Church. **Confirmation** is the sacrament that seals us with the Gift of the Holy Spirit. Like the seal of Baptism, it is always with us. Because of this, we receive Confirmation only once.

During our Confirmation preparation we are also asked to choose a sponsor. A sponsor is a Catholic who has received the Sacraments of Initiation and can help us to grow in faith. Our sponsor stands with us as we receive the Sacrament of Confirmation.

Choosing one of our godparents to be our sponsor again shows the link between Baptism and Confirmation.

The whole parish community prays for those who are to be confirmed. The community gathers with us for the celebration of the sacrament.

Most often a bishop comes to the parish to confirm us. Sometimes a bishop appoints a priest to do the confirming.

The Sacrament of Confirmation is celebrated during Mass, after the Gospel is read and explained.

At Confirmation the bishop asks the same questions asked at Baptism. These are called baptismal promises. They are about our Catholic beliefs.

This is what happens next:

- The bishop talks with us about our faith. He calls us to live lives in service to all. Sometimes he asks us questions, too.

- The bishop and priests celebrating with him stretch out their hands over those receiving the sacrament. The bishop prays to God the Father and asks him to send the Holy Spirit.

- The bishop dips his right thumb in blessed oil. Laying his hands on each person's head, he traces a cross on his or her forehead with the oil. We call this tracing the cross with oil the **anointing with oil**. The bishop prays, "(Person's name), be sealed with the Gift of the Holy Spirit." Then the bishop says "Peace be with you." Those who were confirmed say, "And also with you."

All those gathered join in praying for the Church, the world, and those in need. Then they continue to worship God as the celebration of the Mass continues.

We Respond

At Confirmation, the Holy Spirit brings gifts to us called the gifts of the Holy Spirit. These gifts will help us to respond to God's love, to follow Jesus, and to grow closer to the Holy Spirit.

The Seven Gifts of the Holy Spirit

The gift of	will help us to
Wisdom	see and follow God's will
Understanding	love others as Jesus asks us to
Right Judgment	make good choices
Courage	witness to our faith in Jesus Christ
Knowledge	learn more about God and his plan
Reverence	love and respect all that God has created
Wonder and Awe	see God's presence and love everywhere

The gift of the Holy Spirit that will help most is . . .

I will use this gift by . . .

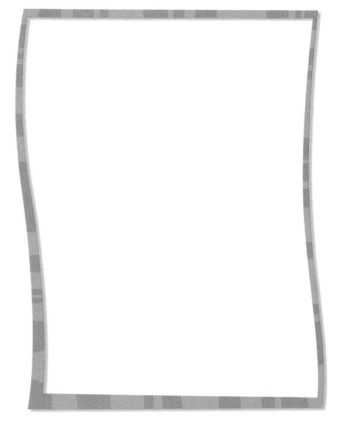

We Respond in Prayer

Leader: In our prayer space we see the red cloth. At Confirmation, the bishop or priest will wear red vestments because red is the color for the Holy Spirit. We also have some perfumed oil like the oil that will be used to anoint us in Confirmation. And we have a bowl of water to remind us of our baptism. Let us bless ourselves using this water as we pray the Sign of the Cross together.

All: In the name of the Father,
and of the Son,
and of the Holy Spirit.
Amen.

Reader: Saint Paul says in his letter to the Galatians, "The fruit of the Spirit is love, joy, peace, patience, kindness, generosity, faithfulness, gentleness, self-control." (Galatians 5:22–23)

Leader: Father, in your great love
you sent Jesus to save us.

All: Thank you.

Leader: Jesus, in your great love
you sent us your Spirit.

All: Thank you.

Leader: Holy Spirit, in you great love
you bring us your gifts.

All: Thank you.

Leader: Let us join in singing "We Believe,
We Believe in God."

We Believe & Celebrate
Catechesis for Older Children

Overview

Older children who are preparing to celebrate First Penance and First Communion need an approach tailored to their situation and needs. The following pages provide resources for involving them in the overall parish process for sacramental preparation while being attentive to these needs. Here are some strategies for effective catechesis and celebration.

Lessons

Pages 75–84 contain a lesson for First Penance and a lesson for First Communion. These lessons contain all the information found in the *We Believe & Celebrate* program and can be offered to a group of older children in the parish or used by parents to catechize their children at home. This material allows parish directors to involve the older children in the overall program for sacramental preparation while also providing individualized catechesis. Used in conjunction with the *Gather In My Name* events and the regular catechetical program, older children can prepare to celebrate First Penance and First Communion in a manner appropriate to their age and readiness.

Keepsake Pages Online

Older children, capable of working independently, will enjoy the option of creating keepsake albums of their own, complete with lessons, reflections, and mementoes of the preparation process and celebration of the sacraments. To start the keepsake album, provide each child with a binder. Decorate the cover. If there are experienced scrapbookers in the parish, enlist their help. Copy the lessons in this book for each child's scrapbook. Then download activities, scrapbook pages, and handouts at www.webelieveandcelebrate.com.

Gather In My Name Events

These intergenerational events are perfectly suited to the preparation of older children. They allow for catechesis within the context of the whole community while also providing options for age-appropriate breakout sessions. The four *GIMN* events in this guide offer opportunities for older children to be given special responsibilities or recognition, thus setting them apart from the "little kids." Incorporate the presentation of keepsake albums into the first *GIMN* events when the younger children receive their keepsake books.

Readiness Meeting for Older Children

Even if you do not offer Readiness Meetings for younger children, it is helpful to provide them for older children, who are more sophisticated thinkers and are bound to have questions or concerns about the sacraments. For more information about these meetings, visit our web site.

The Celebration

Some older children might feel self-conscious about celebrating First Penance or First Communion with a large group of younger children. If your main parish celebration is a large group format, you may want to offer families with older children a small group or household option (see page 35). If younger and older children celebrate the sacrament together, devise activities and responsibilities for older children. Invite them to serve as greeters, to lead processions, or to read intercessions. If you recruit a child to be a lector, you must inspire them to proclaim the Scriptures as well or better than the regular lector. Set the standard high.

 ONLINE COMPONENTS
Visit www.webelieveandcelebrate.com

Planning for Older Children

First Penance	First Communion
Invite children and their families to the "Forgiving Hearts" *Gather In My Name* event.	Invite children and their families to the "Memories of Jesus" *Gather In My Name* event.
Schedule First Penance lesson for parish groups or provide materials for parents to use at home.	Schedule First Communion lesson for parish groups or provide materials for parents to use at home.
Schedule Readiness Meetings and a walk-through of the sacrament, excluding the confession of sins.	Schedule Readiness Meetings and rehearsal for the sacramental celebration.
Invite children and their families to the "Go in Peace" *Gather In My Name* event.	Invite children and their families to the "Recognizing Jesus" *Gather In My Name* event.
Celebrate First Penance with younger children or plan a separate celebration.	Celebrate First Communion with younger children or plan a separate celebration.

FIRST PENANCE

The Ten Commandments

God gave special laws to his people because he loved them and wanted them to be safe and happy. These laws are the **Ten Commandments**. (See handout "The Ten Commandments" at www.webelieveandcelebrate.com.) When Jesus was growing up, he learned the Ten Commandments. He lived by these laws all during his life on earth. He showed us how to follow these laws and how to love God, ourselves, and others.

The following are ways we can show our love for God by following commandments 1–3.

✦ We believe that there is only one God.

✦ We speak God's name only with love and respect.

✦ We join our parish each week for Mass on Sunday or Saturday evening. We take time to rest and enjoy our family and friends.

The following are ways we can show love for ourselves and others by following commandments 4–10.

✦ We listen to and obey our parents and all those who care for us.

✦ We respect all human life; we do not fight or hurt anyone.

✦ We respect our own bodies and the bodies of others.

✦ We take care of what we have. We do not steal from others.

✦ We tell the truth.

✦ We show that we are thankful for our family and friends.

✦ We show that we are thankful for what we have and we share what we have with others.

The Great Commandment

When Jesus was asked which commandment is the greatest, he replied, "You shall love the Lord, your God, with all your heart, with all your soul, and with all your mind" (Matthew 22:37). Then he said, "You shall love your neighbor as yourself" (Matthew 22:29). Jesus' teaching to love God, ourselves, and others is called the **Great Commandment**. When we follow the Great Commandment, we follow all of God's commandments and live as God's children.

Although God wants us to choose to obey his laws as Jesus taught us to do, God never forces us to obey his commandments. God gives us the gift of **free will**. God lets us use our free will to follow his laws or not to follow his laws. God allows us to choose to love and respect him, ourselves, and others. God has also given us a gift to help us make the right choices. Our **conscience** helps us to know what is right and what is wrong, what to do and what not to do. Our conscience helps us to obey God's commandments.

Sometimes people choose to turn away from God's love. They decide not to follow God's law—a choice that hurts their friendship with God. But it is important to remember that God always loves us and is always ready to forgive us if we are sorry. God always gives us the grace to do what he commands and we can always pray to God the Holy Spirit to help us make the right choices.

Sin and Grace

God loves each of us very much. He wants us to stay as close to him as possible, but this is not always easy to do. The first humans sinned and lost their share in God's life. That first sin is called **original sin** and ever since then, all people have been born with original sin. Because of original sin, suffering and death came into the world. Also, people sometimes find it difficult to do what God wants.

Sometimes we do not show our love for God, ourselves, and others. We choose not to obey God's commandments. We sin. **Sin** is any thought, word, or act that we freely choose to commit even though we know that it is wrong. When we sin we turn away from God and one another. But Jesus leads us by showing us ways to come back together again.

Jesus said, "I am the good shepherd" (John 10:14). Jesus, our Good Shepherd, leads us to reconciliation with God and others. The word *reconciliation* comes from a word that means "coming back together again."

Jesus gives us ways to receive God's forgiveness. The first way we receive and celebrate God's forgiveness is in the Sacrament of Baptism. We are either placed in water, or water is poured over us. We receive a share in God's life. God's life in us is **grace**. In Baptism original sin and all other sins are taken away. Through the waters of Baptism, we become children of God and members of the Church.

After we are baptized, there are many times in our lives when we need to ask God to forgive us. We can do this in the Sacrament of Penance and Reconciliation. In this sacrament, which we can call the Sacrament of Penance, we ask God for and receive his forgiveness of our sins.

Some sins are more serious than others. These are called **mortal sins**. To commit a mortal sin, a person knows it is very seriously wrong and freely chooses to commit it anyway. People who commit mortal sin break their friendship with God. They no longer share in God's grace. People who commit mortal sins must receive God's forgiveness in the Sacrament of Penance.

Venial sin is less serious than mortal sin. People who commit venial sin hurt their friendship with God, but they still share in God's grace. Yet any sin that we commit hurts our friendship with God and others, so we should ask for God's forgiveness for all of our sins in the Sacrament of Penance.

An Examination of Conscience

Jesus' parable of the Prodigal Son (Luke 15:11–24) demonstrates God's love and forgiveness. In the story, a man had two sons. One day, the younger son asked his father for his inheritance. His father gave him his share of the money, and the son set off and quickly wasted all of his money. Soon, he found himself alone, poor and hungry. When the son thought about his selfish choices and remembered his father's love, he decided to return home and ask forgiveness from his father. The father welcomed his lost son home and celebrated his return with a feast.

The prodigal son was neither happy nor peaceful. After he spent all his money, he realized the choices he had made were selfish. We, too, should think about whether or not our choices show love for God, ourselves, and others. When we do this we make an **examination of conscience**.

As we prepare to celebrate the Sacrament of Penance, we make an examination of conscience. When we make an examination of conscience, we ask the Holy Spirit to help us remember the choices we have made. We think about the ways we have or have not followed the Ten Commandments. We ask ourselves questions to help us remember what we have thought, said, or done. And we ask ourselves if there were times we could have done good for others but did not.

Here are some questions you can ask when you examine your conscience.

Respect for God
◆ Did I take time to pray?
◆ Did I speak God's name in the right way?

Respect for Myself
◆ Did I take care of my body?
◆ Did I give thanks for all the gifts God has given me?

Respect for Others
◆ Did I obey my parents and all those who care for me?
◆ Did I hurt other people by what I said or did?
◆ Did I look for ways to help others?

In Jesus' story about the father and son, the son felt sorrow for the wrong choices he had made. Another word for sorrow is *contrition*. During the Sacrament of Penance, we pray a special prayer, an *act of contrition*, to tell God that we are sorry for the wrong choices we have made. You can prepare for the sacrament by learning this prayer.

Act of Contrition

My God,
I am sorry for my sins with all my heart.
In choosing to do wrong
and failing to do good,
I have sinned against you
whom I should love above all things.
I firmly intend, with your help,
to do penance,
to sin no more,
and to avoid whatever leads me to sin.
Our Savior Jesus Christ
suffered and died for us.
In his name, my God, have mercy.

Celebrating the Sacrament of Penance

When Jesus traveled from town to town, he met and shared God's love and forgiveness with many people. He also forgave people's sins. He celebrated their reconciliation with God and others. Jesus also gave us a way to celebrate our reconciliation with God and others. He gave us the Sacrament of Penance.

When we celebrate the Sacrament of Penance, we meet with a priest acting in Jesus' name. We may sit and face the priest, or we may kneel behind a screen. The priest may read a story from the Bible with us. Then he talks to us about what we can do to make right choices.

In the Sacrament of Penance we tell God that we are sorry for our sins and we promise not to sin again. This is **contrition**. Perfect contrition is being sorry for our sins because we believe in God and love him. When we tell our sins to the priest, we confess our sins. This part of the sacrament is called **confession**. The priest will never tell anyone the sins that we confess. During this sacrament, the priest tells us ways we can show God we are sorry. The priest may tell us to say an extra prayer or prayers. He may tell us to do kind acts for others. A prayer or kind act we do to show God we are sorry is **a penance**.

The Gospel story of Zacchaeus (Luke 19:1–10) is about a rich tax collector with a reputation for cheating. Zacchaeus promised Jesus that he would show God he was sorry for his sins. He promised to pay back four times the amount of money he owed to people and give half of what he owned to people in need. Jesus told Zacchaeus that he was saved. We, too, show God that we are sorry for our sins by doing the penance that the priest gives us. We usually do the penance after the celebration of the sacrament.

After Jesus rose from the dead, he returned to his Apostles and gave them the power to forgive sin in his name. And today, in the Sacrament of Penance, bishops and priests forgive our sins in Jesus' name. They received this power in the Sacrament of Holy Orders. God forgives our sins through the words and actions of the priest in the Sacrament of Penance. This is called **absolution**. The word *absolution* comes from a word that means "taking away."

When the priest gives absolution, he stretches his right hand over each person's head and prays:

"God, the Father of mercies,
through the death and resurrection of his Son
has reconciled the world to himself
and sent the Holy Spirit among us
for the forgiveness of sins;
through the ministry of the Church
may God give you pardon and peace,
and I absolve you from your sins
in the name of the Father, and of the Son, †
and of the Holy Spirit."

We each respond, "Amen."

Celebrating the Sacrament with the Parish Community

We all need God's forgiveness and love, so our parish community often gathers to celebrate the Sacrament of Penance together.

◆ We sing a song together and then are welcomed by the priest.

◆ We listen to readings from the Bible about God's love and forgiveness.

◆ The priest talks to us about the readings.

◆ We listen to questions that are part of an examination of conscience and think about the choices we have made.

◆ We say an act of contrition together, telling God we are sorry for our sins and that we will try not to sin again. Then together we pray the Our Father.

◆ Each person goes alone to tell his or her sins to the priest.

◆ The priest gives a penance to each person.

◆ Each person receives absolution. The priest stretches his right hand over each person's head and says the words of absolution. In God's name each person's sins are forgiven by the priest.

◆ Together we all praise and thank God for his mercy.

◆ The priest blesses the parish community and tells all of us to "Go in peace."

Celebrating the Sacrament Individually

Sometimes you will celebrate the Sacrament of Penance individually with the priest.

✦ The priest welcomes you, and you both make the sign of the cross.

✦ You listen as the priest shares a Bible story about God's forgiveness.

✦ You confess your sins to the priest.

✦ You and the priest talk about making right choices.

✦ The priest gives a penance to you. You will do your penance after the celebration of the sacrament.

✦ You pray an act of contrition. You tell God you are sorry for your sins and that you will try not to sin again.

✦ You receive absolution. The priest stretches his right hand over your head and says the words of absolution. In God's name your sins are forgiven by the priest.

✦ You and the priest praise and thank God for his love and forgiveness.

✦ The priest tells you, "Go in peace."

Go in Peace

At the end of the celebration of the Sacrament of Penance, the priest tells us, "Go in peace." We go in peace because we have been forgiven. Then as soon as we can, we do the penance the priest has given us. The penance may be to say a prayer or prayers or to do a kind act. When we do a penance, we show that we are sorry for our sins.

Through the Sacrament of Penance:

✦ we are filled with God's grace

✦ we are joined to God and the Church

✦ God takes away punishment for our sins

✦ we receive peace and comfort

✦ we are strengthened to love God.

On the night before he died, Jesus said, "Peace I leave with you; my peace I give to you" (John 14:27). On that same night, Jesus also promised his disciples that the Holy Spirit would come to be our Helper. The Holy Spirit came to the Church on Pentecost. God the Holy Spirit is with the Church to guide us and help people of all ages to make loving, peaceful choices.

FIRST COMMUNION

The Church

A community is a group of people who share, celebrate, and work with one another. The first community we belong to is our family. When we are baptized, we become a part of another community, the Church. The **Church** is all the people who are baptized in Jesus Christ and follow his teachings. Through our Baptism, we belong to the Catholic Church.

As Catholics, we believe in the Blessed Trinity. The Blessed Trinity is three Persons in one God, God the Father, God the Son, and God the Holy Spirit. We believe that Jesus Christ, the Son of God, became one of us and died and rose again to save us. We try to love God and others as Jesus did. We do this through the help of the Holy Spirit.

There are members of the Catholic Church all over the world. Catholics gather together as parish communities to worship God and to share and celebrate God's love. As Catholics we gather together in our parish community for Mass and the celebration of the sacraments. We gather to show our love for God and others.

The Sacraments of Initiation

A **sacrament** is a special sign given to us by Jesus. Every time we celebrate a sacrament, Jesus is with us through the power of the Holy Spirit. The prayers we pray and the things we do show that we are joined, or united, with Jesus, so through each sacrament we share in God's own life and love.

Through Baptism, God shares his life with us. We become children of God and members of the Church. Baptism is the first sacrament we receive. At Baptism, we are placed in water or water is poured over our heads. The priest or deacon prays special words. We are baptized in the name of the Father, and of the Son, and of the Holy Spirit. When we are baptized, we are anointed with oil, reminding us that we are receiving the Gift of the Holy Spirit for the first time.

In the Sacrament of Confirmation, we are sealed with the Gift of the Holy Spirit and strengthened. At Confirmation we are again anointed with oil. This shows that the Holy Spirit is with us in a very special way and that we are set apart to do God's work. In the Sacrament of the Eucharist, the bread and wine become the Body and Blood of Jesus Christ. We receive Jesus Christ himself in Holy Communion. We are united with Jesus Christ and to one another.

Baptism, Confirmation, and Eucharist are the Sacraments of Initiation. Another word for initiation is *beginning*. After we receive all three of these sacraments, we are full members of the Church.

The Mass

We gather with our parish community to celebrate God's love and worship God together. To **worship** God means "to praise and thank" him. Every Sunday we gather with our parish to worship God. We celebrate the Eucharist. This celebration of the Eucharist is called the **Mass**. By our special words and actions, we show that we believe that God is with us.

The community of people who join together for the celebration of the Mass is called the gathered **assembly**. A priest leads the gathered assembly in this celebration as the celebrant. He is often assisted by a deacon. At Mass the priest and the deacon wear special clothing called vestments.

Throughout the Mass we show God our love by singing, praying, and listening to God's word. Together with the priest, we

+ praise and thank God
+ listen to God's word
+ remember Jesus' life, death, Resurrection, and Ascension
+ celebrate that Jesus gives himself to us in the Eucharist.

The Parts of the Mass

Introductory Rites

The celebration of Mass begins with the Introductory Rites. These prayers and actions at the beginning of the Mass help us to remember that we are a worshiping community. They prepare us to listen to God's word and to celebrate the Eucharist. Here is what we do during the Introductory Rites:

+ We stand and sing to praise God. As we sing, the priest, deacon, and others helping at Mass walk to the altar. The priest and deacon kiss the altar as a sign of respect.

+ We make the sign of the cross. Then the priest greets us. His words and our response remind us that Jesus is present with us.

+ The priest asks us to think about times we have not loved God and others. Then we ask God and one another for forgiveness.

+ Together with the priest we praise God for his love and forgiveness. We pray:
  "Lord, have mercy.
  Christ, have mercy.
  Lord, have mercy."

+ We often sing or say a prayer of praise to God the Father, God the Son, and God the Holy Spirit. This prayer begins with the words:
  "Glory to God in the highest,
  and peace to his people on earth."

+ The priest prays an opening prayer. We respond, "Amen."

Liturgy of the Word

The Bible is the book of God's word. The Bible has two parts, the Old Testament and the New Testament. In the Old Testament we learn about God's people who lived before Jesus' time on earth. In the New Testament we learn about Jesus and his disciples and about the beginning of the Church.

Every Sunday at Mass we listen to three readings from the Bible. We listen to God speaking to us through his word. This takes place during the Liturgy of the Word. The **Liturgy of the Word** is the part of the Mass in which we listen to God's word being proclaimed. To *proclaim* means "to announce God's word."

On most Sundays the first reading is from the Old Testament. From this reading we learn about the wonderful things God did for his people before Jesus was born. We learn that God's love for his people never ends. A **psalm** is a song of praise from the Bible. After the first reading the reader or cantor prays a psalm verse. We sing or say a response.

The second reading is from the New Testament. During this reading we listen to the teachings of the Apostles and learn about the beginning of the Church.

The third reading is the **Gospel reading**. It is from one of the four Gospels of the New Testament. The word *gospel* means "good news." On most Sundays we sing Alleluia before the Gospel is read. When we listen to the Gospel, we learn the Good News about Jesus Christ and his teachings.

We praise and thank God during the Liturgy of the Word. We pray, "Thanks be to God," after the first and second readings. We pray, "Praise to you, Lord Jesus Christ," after the Gospel.

After we have heard all the readings, the priest or deacon talks to us about them. This talk is called the **homily**. When we listen carefully to the homily, we learn more about God and ways we can share God's love with others. When the homily is finished, we pray the **creed**. We announce what we believe as Catholics. We believe in God the Father, God the Son, and God the Holy Spirit. We believe in the Church and in God's forgiveness of our sins.

After the creed we pray the **prayer of the faithful**. Sometimes this is called the *general intercessions*. We pray for the needs of all God's people. We pray for the whole Church. We pray for the pope, other Church leaders, and all God's people throughout the world, especially for those who are sick or in need. We pray for the people in our parish who have died and for people in our lives who need God's love and help. After each prayer, we ask God to hear our prayer.

Liturgy of the Eucharist

Jesus told his disciples to remember what he had done at the Last Supper. He told them to remember and celebrate this special meal again and again. He said, "Do this in memory of me" (Luke 22:19). We do what Jesus asked each time we celebrate the Eucharist. The Mass is the celebration of the Eucharist. The word *eucharist* means "to give thanks." Throughout the Mass, we give God thanks and praise.

The **Liturgy of the Eucharist** is the part of the Mass in which the bread and wine become the Body and Blood of Jesus Christ. The Liturgy of the Eucharist begins as the priest prepares the altar. Then members of the assembly bring forward the gifts of bread and wine. We remember the many gifts God has given to us. We get ready to offer these gifts and ourselves back to God. The word *offer* means "to give" or "to present."

The priest or deacon accepts the gifts of bread and wine. He brings them to the altar. He prepares the gifts with special prayers. We respond, "Blessed be God for ever." Then we pray with the priest that the Lord will accept these gifts.

Throughout the Liturgy of the Eucharist, we remember that the Mass is a **sacrifice**, or an offering of a gift to God. As a sacrifice, Jesus offered his life for us on the cross to save us from sin. He rose to new life so that we could live happily with God forever. At every Mass, Jesus again offers himself to the Father. The Eucharist is offered to make up for the sins of the living and the dead. Through it we receive spiritual and physical help from God.

After the gifts are prepared, we pray the Eucharistic Prayer. The **Eucharistic Prayer** is the great prayer of praise and thanksgiving. This prayer is the most important prayer of the Church. It joins the members of the Church to Christ and to one another. The priest prays the Eucharistic Prayer in the name of the whole Church. He prays to God the Father through Jesus Christ in the Holy Spirit.

Through the power of the Holy Spirit the priest says and does what Jesus said and did at the Last Supper. Taking the bread the priest says:

"Take this, all of you, and eat it: this is my body which will be given up for you."

Then taking the cup of wine he says:

"Take this, all of you, and drink from it: this is the cup of my blood. . . ."

This part of the Eucharistic Prayer is called the **consecration**. By the power of the Holy Spirit and through the words and actions of the priest, the bread and wine become the Body and Blood of Christ. Jesus Christ is really present in the Eucharist. We call this the *Real Presence.* The priest invites us to proclaim our faith. We may pray:

"Christ has died,
Christ is risen,
Christ will come again."

We pray that the Holy Spirit will unite all who believe in Jesus. We end the Eucharistic Prayer by praying "Amen." When we do this, we are saying "Yes, I believe." We are saying "yes" to the prayer the priest has prayed in our name.

In the Liturgy of the Eucharist, after the Eucharistic Prayer, we prepare to receive Jesus himself in Holy Communion. Our gifts of bread and wine have now become the Body and Blood of Christ. And we will receive the Body and Blood of Christ in Holy Communion. We join ourselves with the whole Church as we pray aloud or sing the Lord's Prayer. Then the priest reminds us of Jesus' words at the Last Supper.

Jesus said, "Peace I leave with you; my peace I give to you" (John 14:27). We pray that Christ's peace may be with us always. We share a sign of peace with the people near us. When we do this we show that we are united to Jesus Christ and to one another.

After we share a sign of peace, we pray to Jesus who sacrificed his life to save us from sin. We ask him for forgiveness and peace. We begin the prayer with these words:
"Lamb of God, you take away
	the sins of the world:
	have mercy on us."

As we pray the Lamb of God, the priest breaks the Bread, the Host, that has become the Body of Christ. After we pray the Lamb of God, the priest invites us to receive Jesus Christ in Holy Communion. The priest says,
"This is the Lamb of God
	who takes away the sins of the world.
Happy are those who are called to his supper."
Together with the priest we pray,
	"Lord, I am not worthy to receive you,
	but only say the word and I shall be healed."

Then we go forward with love and respect to receive Jesus in Holy Communion. As each person approaches, the priest, deacon, or extraordinary minister of Holy Communion raises the Host. The person bows his or her head. The priest, deacon, or extraordinary minister says, "The Body of Christ." The person responds "Amen" and then receives the Host. If the person is receiving from the chalice, the priest, deacon, or extraordinary minister of Holy Communion raises the chalice. The person bows his or her head. The priest, deacon, or extraordinary minister says, "The Blood of Christ." The person responds, "Amen" and drinks from the cup.

As the gathered assembly receives the Body and Blood of Christ, we sing a song of thanksgiving. We are united with the whole Church. During the quiet time that follows, we remember that Jesus is present within us and thank Jesus for the gift of himself in Holy Communion.

The Concluding Rites

Jesus sent his disciples out to continue his work. As his disciples, Jesus wants us to keep doing his work, too. He wants us to share God's love with others in our homes, schools, parishes, neighborhoods, cities or towns, and throughout the world. God's grace helps us to do all that he asks.

The celebration of the Mass ends with the **Concluding Rites**. At the end of Mass, together with the priest, we ask the Lord to be with us. Then the priest gives us a blessing. He says, "May almighty God bless you, the Father, and the Son, † and the Holy Spirit."
We respond, "Amen."

Then the priest or deacon sends us out to share God's love with others. He may say, "Go in peace to love and serve the Lord." We respond, "Thanks be to God."

We sing a song as everyone leaves the church. All through the week we remember Jesus' promise to be with us always. Every Sunday we are joined to Jesus and the whole Church in the Sacrament of the Eucharist. We receive Jesus in Holy Communion, and our friendship with him grows. Our venial sins are forgiven and we are helped to stay away from serious sin.

Through the Holy Spirit, Jesus is with us as we continue his work all through the week. Receiving Jesus in Holy Communion helps us to love God and others. We become stronger disciples of Jesus. This helps us to join our parish community in loving and serving God and others in many ways: by helping out at home or in school, doing something kind for a friend or neighbor, giving to a food or clothing drive, visiting someone who is sick, praying for others, especially poor or hungry, and forgiving others or asking for their forgiveness.

CHAPTER 1

Home Lesson Plan

Introduce the Chapter *(page 7)*

Light a candle. Pray the Sign of the Cross and read the Scripture verse on page 7.

Look at the photograph of the family. Discuss the ways family members might show their love for one another.

STEP 1

We Gather *(pages 8–9)*

Read the story about Dan and Grandma Lynn. Discuss ways Grandma Lynn showed Dan that she loved him. Help your child write what Dan's response to his grandmother might be.

Talk with your child about the people who care for and protect him or her. Help your child draw a picture of and write about one of the persons named.

We Share God's Word *(pages 10–11)*

Explain that God gave us laws because he loves us and wants to protect us. Explain that God's laws are called commandments. Then read the *Narrator* paragraphs.

Read the Scripture story about Jesus' teaching. Emphasize that we follow all God's commandments when we follow the Great Commandment by showing love for God, ourselves, and others.

STEP 2

We Believe and Celebrate *(pages 12–13)*

Explain that God's laws are the Ten Commandments. Read the second paragraph on page 12. At this time you may want to read the Ten Commandments on page 79.

Read the ways we show our love for God when we follow the first, second, and third commandments. Discuss ways your family can rest on Sundays and enjoy time together.

Look at the photos on page 13 as you read aloud the list of ways we follow the fourth through the tenth commandments.

Read the last paragraph on page 13. Stress that when we follow the Great Commandment we follow all of God's commandments. Then discuss how the children in the photos on pages 12 and 13 are following the Great Commandment.

We Believe and Celebrate *(pages 14–15)*

Point out to your child that God wants us to choose to love him, ourselves, and others. He has given us two gifts to help us to do this.

Read aloud the text on page 14, the first paragraph on page 15, and the feature *Making Choices*. Emphasize God's gifts of free will and conscience. Explain that learning about ways to follow God's commandments helps us to develop our conscience.

Emphasize that God never forces us to obey his commandments. Then read aloud the last two paragraphs on page 15. Ask your child to highlight or underline the second sentence in the last paragraph: *God is always ready to forgive us if we are sorry.*

Write a short prayer together, asking the Holy Spirit to guide you in making right choices.

STEP 3

We Respond *(pages 16–17)*

Help your child recall ways we show our love for God by following the first three commandments. Then read aloud the text at the top of page 16. Explain that the activity may be completed by drawing a picture and/or writing. Point out that joining our parish for Mass on Sunday or Saturday evening is the most important way.

Discuss ways that your family can show respect for one another and for your neighbors. Then read each sentence starter on page 17. Invite your child to write about or draw a picture to tell about one way for each category.

We Respond in Prayer *(page 18)*

Set up a prayer space. Place a small table in the space. On the table place a candle, a cross or crucifix, and a Bible.

Pray the Sign of the Cross together. Take the role of Leader and invite your child to pray the responses. Sing together "We Celebrate with Joy," #1 on the *We Believe & Celebrate* CD.

Complete the *Sharing Faith with My Family* activities for Chapter 1 on pages 81–82 of the child's text.

We Believe & Celebrate First Penance

Introduce the Chapter *(page 19)*

Light a candle. Pause for a moment and invite reflection about God's gifts of love and forgiveness. Proclaim together the psalm verse on page 19.

Explain that the psalm writer called God his shepherd because the writer believed that God loved and cared for his people, like a shepherd for his sheep.

STEP 1

We Gather *(pages 20–21)*

Read the story. Discuss how Marta got separated from her family, how they were reunited, and what Mr. Cruz told Marta. Discuss ways the family could celebrate being together again. Then help your child write an ending for the story.

Talk about favorite family activities. Have your child illustrate and/or write about one activity in the space on page 21.

We Share God's Word *(pages 22–23)*

Explain that shepherds took care of about one hundred sheep at a time. They tried to watch out so that individual sheep did not wander too far from the flock.

Read aloud the Gospel story and the last paragraph. Then look together at the illustration on page 23; talk about the trouble the shepherd took to find the lost sheep. Invite your child to tell how the shepherd felt after finding it.

STEP 2

We Believe and Celebrate *(pages 24–25)*

Read aloud the first two paragraphs on page 24. Keep your explanation of original sin as simple as it is in the second paragraph.

Read aloud the third paragraph on page 24. Emphasize that we sin only when we choose to do something wrong or do it on purpose. Explain that mistakes and accidents are not sins.

Look at the picture of Jesus, the Good Shepherd. Stress how wonderful it is that Jesus leads us to reconciliation with God and others.

Look at the photo of the Baptism of the infant. Stress that it is at Baptism that we receive God's life in us, grace. In Baptism, original sin and all other sins are taken away.

We Believe and Celebrate *(pages 26–27)*

Remind your child that we first receive God's forgiveness at Baptism. Point out that we also celebrate God's forgiveness in another sacrament. Then read aloud the first paragraph on page 26.

Emphasize that God is always ready to forgive us if we are sorry before reading the second paragraph on page 26.

Read the two paragraphs on page 27. Point out that people who commit venial sin hurt their friendship with God, but they still share in God's grace.

Read the names for the Sacrament of Penance as presented in the *When We Celebrate* feature on page 27. Also read the paragraph following these names.

STEP 3

We Respond *(pages 28–29)*

Remind your child about Jesus' story of the shepherd and the lost sheep. Help your child name other stories told by Jesus or about Jesus that help us understand God's forgiveness. Then invite your child to draw a picture of or write about one of these stories.

Read the sentence at the top of page 29. Invite your child to draw a picture of Jesus, our Good Shepherd, on the left side of the space provided. Then on the right side write your family prayer.

We Respond in Prayer *(page 30)*

Set on the prayer table a bowl of holy water, a cross, and a Bible.

Invite each person to dip his or her fingers in the holy water and then pray the Sign of the Cross. Lead the prayer and the singing of "The Good Shepherd," #2 on the *We Believe & Celebrate* CD.

Complete the *Sharing Faith with My Family* activities on pages 83–84 of the child's text.

Introduce the Chapter *(page 31)*

Light a candle and pray together the Sign of the Cross. Read aloud the verse on page 31.

Look at the family photograph. Point out that everyone looks happy and peaceful. Talk about a peaceful and pleasant time your family has shared.

STEP 1

We Gather *(pages 32–33)*

Read aloud the story about Andrew and his sister. Discuss the choice that Andrew made. (Because he was angry, he took Lisa's shell.) Talk about what Andrew might say to apologize. Then have your child write these words to complete the story.

Have your child draw a self-portrait below the story. Draw a speech bubble beside the picture. Discuss ways to tell people we are sorry. Help your child write one way in the bubble.

We Share God's Word *(pages 34–35)*

Read aloud the first sentence on page 34 and the story. Point out that the son in the story stands for all of us, whenever we sin and ask for God's forgiveness. Point out that the father reminds us of God the Father who is always happy when we choose to say that we are sorry and come back to him by asking him to forgive us.

Work together to prepare a dramatic presentation of the story. Share the play with family and friends.

STEP 2

We Believe and Celebrate *(pages 36–37)*

Help your child identify choices that involve choosing whether or not to follow God's commandments.

Remind your child that our gift of conscience helps us to know right from wrong. Then read aloud the first two paragraphs on page 36. You may want to point out that our study of Jesus' teachings helps us to form our conscience so that we know right from wrong.

Read aloud the four things we do when we make an examination of conscience. Explain that examining one's conscience requires quiet and serious "thinking and praying time."

Read the questions on page 37, pausing after each one to allow your child to reflect on his or her response.

We Believe and Celebrate *(pages 38–39)*

Remind your child that the father and the son in Jesus' story used words of sorrow and forgiveness to make peace. Then read the text on page 38. Explain that we pray an act of contrition during the Sacrament of Penance and at other times when we are sorry for our sins and want to ask God to forgive us.

Read the Act of Contrition on page 39. Explain that this is one version of the prayer. Point out that we can always use our own words to tell God that we are sorry.

Read the feature *When We Pray*. Then read the prayer aloud together. Pray this Act of Contrition (or another preferred version) together often before the celebration of your child's First Penance.

STEP 3

We Respond *(pages 40–41)*

Invite your child to complete the first sentence by drawing a picture of and/or writing about a favorite place for an examination of conscience.

Discuss times when a person can make an examination of conscience (during nighttime prayers, before celebrating the Sacrament of Penance). Help your child complete the second sentence on page 40 by drawing or writing.

Write together a family plan for showing respect for God, self, and others.

We Respond in Prayer *(page 42)*

Remind your child that Jesus wants us to celebrate God's love and forgiveness.

Take the role of Leader and begin the prayer. Pause briefly after praying each line of the Act of Contrition. Then lead the singing of "Children of God," #3 on the *We Believe and Celebrate* CD.

Complete the *Sharing Faith with My Family* activities on pages 85–86 of the child's text.

CHAPTER 4

Home Lesson Plan

Introduce the Chapter (page 43)

Pray together the Sign of the Cross. Invite your child to join you in crossing your arms over your hearts as you pray the prayer verse on page 43.

Look at the photo of the family on page 43. Talk about the ways the parents might guide the children to respect God, themselves, and others.

STEP 1

We Gather (pages 44–45)

Read aloud the story on pages 44 and 45. Discuss what happened between the two friends and how Margaret's mother helped her make things right again. Talk about ways Margaret can show she is sorry. Then have your child write a story ending.

Discuss ways we can show friends that we are sorry. In the space below the story, have your child draw a picture of and/or write about one way.

We Share God's Word (pages 46–47)

Explain that in Jesus' time some tax collectors kept some money for themselves. Then read the story of Zacchaeus. Discuss the story by asking what the words and actions of Zacchaeus showed (he was truly sorry) and what Jesus did for Zacchaeus (forgave him).

Note: You may want to listen to the song "A Man Named Zacchaeus," #8 on the *We Believe & Celebrate* CD.

STEP 2

We Believe and Celebrate (pages 48–49)

Explain that the Church has a special way to share God's love and forgiveness with us. Then read the first two paragraphs on page 48.

Write the words *contrition, confession,* and *a penance* on a sheet of paper. Then read aloud the last paragraph on page 48 and the text on page 49.

Stress that the priest acts in the name of Jesus and that the priest will never tell anyone the sins that we confess.

Point out that, by completing the penance the priest gives us when we celebrate the Sacrament of Penance, we show God that we are truly sorry. We also show God that we never want to sin again.

We Believe and Celebrate (pages 50–51)

Point out that Jesus gave to his Apostles the power to forgive sin in his name. Then read the first paragraph on page 50.

Read aloud the second paragraph on page 50 and the text on page 51. Stress that God's forgiveness of our sins through the words and actions of the priest is called *absolution*. Look at the photo on page 50. Explain that, when the priest gives someone absolution, he extends his right hand over the person's head while saying the words of absolution. Read again these words on page 51.

Look at the image of Jesus on page 51. Explain to your child that one way Jesus watches over us is by sharing God's love and forgiveness with us.

STEP 3

We Respond (pages 52–53)

Read aloud the sentence starter on page 52. Explain: *You can complete the sentence by drawing a picture of and/or writing about what you do or how you feel after being forgiven.*

Discuss ways your family can celebrate forgiveness. Examples might include sharing a special snack or working peacefully on a family project. Invite your child to complete the sentence on page 53 by drawing or writing about your family's celebrations of forgiveness.

We Respond in Prayer (page 54)

Place on the prayer table a candle and a cross or picture of Jesus.

Lead the singing of "Jesus Wants to Help Us," #4 on the *We Believe & Celebrate* CD.

Invite your child to sit comfortably. Explain that you will be praying in the silence of your own hearts. Then read *Quiet Prayer.*

Complete the *Sharing Faith with My Family* activities on pages 87–88 of the child's text.

CHAPTER 5 Home Lesson Plan

Introduce the Chapter (page 55)

Light a candle and read aloud the prayer verse on the page. Explain that to be *merciful* means to shower others with love and forgiveness.

Look at the photo of the family. Stress that our families are part of our parish community with whom we will celebrate the Sacrament of Penance.

STEP 1

We Gather (pages 56–57)

Read aloud the story on page 56. Talk about songs or hymns about God's love and forgiveness. Help your child choose a song and write the title on the line provided on page 56. Then continue reading the story.

Talk about the people who celebrated the Sacrament of Penance with Luz and Marcos. Then read the text below the story. Invite your child to write the names of or draw pictures of some of the people who will celebrate the Sacrament of Penance with him or her.

We Share God's Word (pages 58–59)

Explain that, in the time of Jesus, people wore sandals and walked on dirty, dusty roads. Explain that one of the jobs of wealthy people's servants was to wash the dusty feet of guests as they arrived for special dinners.

Read the story. Help your child conclude that the woman who washed Jesus' feet was crying because she was sorry for her sins. Point out that when Jesus forgave her sins, she must have felt happy and peaceful.

STEP 2

We Believe and Celebrate (pages 60–61)

Help your child recall the four parts of the Sacrament of Penance: contrition, confession, a penance, and absolution. Point out that they are always part of the celebration of Penance.

Present the steps of the communal celebration. You may want to help your child enact the steps except the actual confession of sins.

Look at the photo on page 60 as you read the text of *When We Celebrate*. Also look together at the church illustration on pages 4 and 5 of the child's text. Point out that the illustration shows different places in church where we may confess our sins and receive absolution.

We Believe and Celebrate (pages 62–63)

Point out that the Church has two ways of celebrating the Sacrament of Penance. Read the first sentence on page 62. Explain that the pictures and text on pages 62 and 63 present the steps when we celebrate the sacrament individually with the priest.

Present the steps of the ritual of the sacrament. Then ask what step is shown in each photograph on these pages (page 62: bottom left— priest welcoming child; top right— priest reading a Bible story about God's forgiveness; page 63: child receiving absolution).

Note: At this time you may want to show your child the reconciliation room or confessional in your parish church.

STEP 3

We Respond (pages 64–65)

Ask your child to name the people who have helped him or her prepare for First Penance. Discuss ways to thank these people. Ask your child to draw a picture of or write about one of these ways at the top of page 64. Then write the date for the celebration on the line provided.

Discuss ideas for your family's banner. Consider using Jesus, the Good Shepherd, as a theme. Have your child draw the design on page 65. Then make a felt or paper banner for church or the family prayer space.

We Respond in Prayer (page 66)

Pray the Sign of the Cross and the opening prayer.

Invite careful listening as you play "We Come to Ask Your Forgiveness," #5 on the *We Believe and Celebrate* CD. If the CD is not available, read aloud the words to the song. Explain that walls separate us from other people, but bridges connect us. After the song, share a sign of peace.

Complete the *Sharing Faith with My Family* activities for Chapter 5 on pages 89–90 of the child's text.

We Believe & Celebrate First Penance

Copyright © by William H. Sadlier, Inc. Permission to duplicate classroom quantities granted to users of the *We Believe & Celebrate* Program.

Introduce the Chapter *(page 67)*

Light a candle and read the prayer verse on page 67. Explain that people can be signs because they can point the way to God's love.

Look at the photograph of the family on page 67. Discuss ways family members might be signs of God's love for others.

STEP 1

We Gather *(pages 68–69)*

Talk about the ways our actions can affect the lives of many other people. Read the story and discuss the way two boys' choices affected a whole team.

Help your child write the ending for the story on the lines provided on page 69.

Invite your child to draw pictures and/or write about ways he or she works well together with others in the space provided below the story ending.

We Share God's Word *(pages 70–71)*

Look at the Scripture illustration on pages 70 and 71. Point out that everyone is listening very carefully to what Jesus is telling them.

Read aloud the story and the paragraph that follows. Stress that when we live as peacemakers, we live as signs of God's love and mercy.

STEP 2

We Believe and Celebrate *(pages 72–73)*

Explain that at the end of every celebration of the Sacrament of Penance, the priest tells us to go peacefully. Read aloud the text on page 72. Stress that when we do a penance, we show that we are sorry for our sins.

Look at the illustration on page 73. Explain that the picture shows Saint Francis of Assisi helping people make peace with one another. Read *A Loving Peaceful Saint*. Discuss how Saint Francis was a peacemaker. Pray together the words of the saint: "Lord, make me an instrument of your peace."

We Believe and Celebrate *(pages 74–75)*

Read aloud the first three paragraphs on page 74. Explain: *Jesus knew that it would not be easy for us to forgive and to ask for forgiveness. Jesus asked God the Father to send us a Helper. Our Helper is the Holy Spirit.*

Read the situation on pages 74 and 75. Invite comments and questions about each situation. Then ask your child to share a peaceful choice he or she has made.

Have your child paste a photograph of himself or herself in the marked bead on page 74. If a photograph is not available, have your child draw a self-portrait to place there.

STEP 3

We Respond *(pages 76–77)*

Help your child identify some people who are peacemakers and ways these people share God's gift of peace with others. Explain that the two sentences on page 76 may be completed by drawing and/or writing.

Discuss ways your family can share God's gift of peace. Explain that the sentence on page 77 may be completed by drawing pictures and/or writing. You may also consider taking a photograph of your family sharing peace and affixing it in the space provided.

We Respond in Prayer *(page 78)*

Lead the singing of "God Has Made Us a Family," #6 on the *We Believe & Celebrate* CD.

Consider concluding the prayer celebration by joining hands as you pray together the Lord's Prayer.

Complete the *Sharing Faith with My Family* activities for Chapter 6 on pages 91–92 of the child's text.

Home Lesson Plan

Introduce the Chapter *(page 7)*

Light a candle. Pray the Sign of the Cross and the verse on page 7. Explain that at Baptism we received a lighted candle as a symbol of Christ's life now living within us.

Look at the photograph of the family. Explain that your family is a community—a group of people who share with one another, work together, and care for one another.

STEP 1

We Gather *(pages 8–9)*

Read aloud the sentence on page 8. Help your child complete the sentence by writing your family surname. Ask your child to draw a picture of your family within the frame on page 8, or you may want to paste a family photo there.

Discuss ways you show love for one another. Invite your child to draw a picture of or write about two ways within the frames on page 9.

We Share God's Word *(pages 10–11)*

Remind your child that disciples are followers of Jesus. Jesus and his disciples were a community. Explain that the Scripture story tells what happened to this community about ten days after Jesus returned to his Father in heaven.

Read the story about the Holy Spirit coming to help Jesus' disciples. Explain that on this day, Pentecost Sunday, the Church began.

STEP 2

We Believe and Celebrate *(pages 12–13)*

Present what a community is as described in the first paragraph on page 12. Then read the second paragraph. Stress that at Baptism we become members of the Church community.

Read the next two paragraphs on page 12. Point out that Catholics believe in the Blessed Trinity, the three Persons in one God. Have your child name the three Persons: God the Father, God the Son, and God the Holy Spirit.

Explain that Catholics believe that Jesus Christ, the Son of God, died and rose again to save us.

Present the text on page 13. Emphasize that Catholics gather together in our parish community, especially for the celebration of Mass and the sacraments.

Read the list of the seven sacraments. Stress that Baptism is always the first sacrament a Catholic receives.

We Believe and Celebrate *(pages 14–15)*

Present what a sacrament is as explained in the first paragraph on page 14. Stress that when we celebrate each sacrament, we are united with Jesus.

Look at the photo of the baby being baptized. Stress that at Baptism we receive the gift of God's grace, and we become children of God and members of the Church.

Read the third paragraph on page 14. Explain that the priest or deacon baptizes a person in the name of the Father, and of the Son, and of the Holy Spirit.

Read the text on page 15. Emphasize what happens in the Sacraments of Confirmation and Eucharist. Explain that the Mass is the celebration of the Sacrament of the Eucharist. Point out that when we receive Holy Communion at Mass, we receive the Body and Blood of Jesus Christ.

STEP 3

We Respond *(pages 16–17)*

Help your child fill in the parish names in the appropriate sentences. Discuss things your family can do with your parish community. Then have your child draw a picture of one of these activities in the space provided on page 16.

Read aloud the sentences on page 17. Ask your child to draw pictures and/or write about his or her Baptism and the family helping your child to prepare to receive Jesus in the Eucharist.

We Respond in Prayer *(page 18)*

Prepare to pray. If the *We Believe & Celebrate* CD is available, play "We Believe, We Believe in God," #11 on the CD. If the CD is not available, read aloud together the song words.

Pray the Sign of the Cross together. Take the role of Leader and invite your child to pray the responses.

Complete the *Sharing Faith with My Family* activities for Chapter 1 on pages 81–82 of child's text.

We Believe & Celebrate First Communion

CHAPTER 2

Home Lesson Plan

Introduce the Chapter *(page 19)*

Gather at a window, if possible, and look up at the sky. Proclaim together the verse on page 19. Explain that we pray these same words often at the beginning of Mass.

Look at the photograph of the family. Together make up a story about the ways they might be enjoying their time together in God's world.

STEP 1

We Gather *(pages 20–21)*

Discuss times when your family gathers to celebrate and the reasons you gather. Invite your child to draw pictures and/or write about favorite family celebrations on page 20.

Help your child to choose his or her most special celebration to draw a picture of in the frame at the top of page 21. If you have photos of the celebration, affix them in the space. Then help your child write why the celebration is most special to him or her.

We Share God's Word *(pages 22–23)*

Look together at the illustration on these pages. Explain that the people are welcoming Jesus to Jerusalem. Many Jewish people went to Jerusalem to celebrate some of their feasts. Then read the first two paragraphs on page 22.

Read aloud the Scripture story. Emphasize that the people were praising Jesus in words and honoring him with their actions. Proclaim together the words of praise in Mark 11:9.

STEP 2

We Believe and Celebrate *(pages 24–25)*

Read aloud the first two paragraphs on page 24. Stress that the Mass is the celebration of the Eucharist. At Mass we worship God in words and action.

Call attention to *Our Sunday Celebration* feature. Read the text aloud. Talk about ways you can prepare for Sunday's celebration and ways you can relax on Sundays and enjoy time together as a family.

Present the third paragraph on page 24. Stress that each time you participate in Mass you are part of the gathered assembly. Explain that the priest is the celebrant of the Mass.

Read the *Our Parish Priests* feature on page 25. Stress that the priest acts in the Person of Christ in celebrating Mass and the other sacraments.

Present the four important things we do at Mass by reading the text on page 25.

We Believe and Celebrate *(pages 26–27)*

Call attention to the photograph on page 26. Explain that at the beginning of Mass, altar servers, lectors (readers), and extraordinary ministers of Holy Communion process (walk prayerfully) with the deacon and priest to the altar.

Explain that there are four parts of the Mass: the Introductory Rites, the Liturgy of the Word, the Liturgy of the Eucharist, and the Concluding Rites. Read aloud the first paragraph on page 26. Then talk about what the Introductory Rites help us do.

Read aloud the remaining text on page 26 and the text on page 27. Explain that when we ask God for mercy, we are asking for his forgiveness. Read the "Lord, have mercy" prayer together.

Stress that it is important to participate during the Introductory Rites. By joining others in song and prayer, we show God our love.

STEP 3

We Respond *(pages 28–29)*

Read aloud the first sentence starter on page 28. Help your child write and decorate these words. Explain that the second sentence on page 28 may be completed by drawing pictures of and/or writing about these actions.

Talk about a family prayer space. Help your child complete the activity on page 29 by drawing and/or writing about the space.

We Respond in Prayer *(page 30)*

Prepare to pray. Gather the items needed for the celebration: bowl of holy water, cross, candle. Play "We Celebrate with Joy," #12 on the *We Believe & Celebrate* CD.

Pray the Sign of the Cross. As each item is mentioned in the prayer, place that item on the prayer-space table.

Complete the *Sharing Faith with My Family* activities for Chapter 2 on pages 83–84 of child's text.

Introduce the Chapter *(page 31)*

Place a Bible and a plant or flowers in your prayer space. Proclaim the verse on the page.

Look at the family photograph. Explain that the people in this family enjoy spending time together, listening to each other. Talk about the importance of your family listening to each other.

STEP 1

We Gather *(pages 32–33)*

Read the sentence starters on page 32. Share the names of favorite stories and the reasons why they are favorites. Then ask your child to complete the sentences by drawing and/or writing about his or her favorite story.

Share favorite Bible stories. Read the sentence starters on page 33. Then ask your child to complete the sentences by drawing and/or writing about his or her favorite story.

We Share God's Word *(pages 34–35)*

Explain that the Scripture story you will share is one Jesus told his followers. Jesus used their knowledge about farming to teach about listening to God's Word.

Read the story on page 34. Then explain that the seeds on the path are like people who learn what Jesus taught but cannot accept his message. The seeds on rocky ground are like people who find it too hard to follow Jesus' example. The seeds among thorns and weeds are people who are selfish. Then read the last paragraph. Stress the importance of listening to God's word.

STEP 2

We Believe and Celebrate *(pages 36–37)*

Ask your child what she or he has learned about the Bible. Then read aloud the first paragraph on page 36.

Talk about where and when we listen to God's word. Stress that God's word is proclaimed to us at Mass each Sunday during the Liturgy of the Word.

Look at the photo of the lector on page 36. Explain that the lector, or reader, reads the first two readings at Mass on Sunday. Then read aloud the second and third paragraphs on page 36 and the first two paragraphs on page 37.

Look at the photo of the deacon on page 37. Explain that he is proclaiming the Gospel. Explain that we stand as we listen to the Gospel because Jesus Christ is present in his word and is speaking to us. Read the last two paragraphs on page 37.

We Believe and Celebrate *(pages 38–39)*

Stress the importance of listening and responding to God's Word at Mass. Then read aloud the first paragraph on page 38.

Explain that after we listen to the readings, the priest or deacon talks to us about them. This talk is called a homily.

Read about the creed in the third paragraph on page 38. Share the creeds found on pages 93 and 94 of the child's text.

Explain that after the creed we pray for the needs of all God's people. Then read the last paragraph on page 38 and the paragraph on page 39.

Present *When We Celebrate* on page 39. At Mass next Sunday, point out the *Lectionary* and the *Book of the Gospels.*

STEP 3

We Respond *(pages 40–41)*

Talk about ways we praise and thank God during the Liturgy of the Word. Also discuss people whom your child would like to pray for at next Sunday's Mass. Explain that both sentences on page 40 can be completed by writing and/or drawing.

Explain that the activity on page 41 can be completed by drawing pictures of your family living out God's word.

We Respond in Prayer *(page 42)*

Prepare to pray. In your prayer space, place a plant. On the prayer table place an open Bible.

Pray the Sign of the Cross together. Lead the prayer. Join in singing "Take the Word of God with You," #13 on the *We Believe & Celebrate* CD.

Complete the *Sharing Faith with My Family* activities for Chapter 3 on pages 85–86 of child's text.

Introduce the Chapter (page 43)

Light a candle. Pray the Sign of the Cross and the call to thanks on page 43. Talk with your child about the gifts God has given us.

Look at the photograph of the family. Share a memory of your family preparing for a special meal. What did you do to prepare for it?

STEP 1

We Gather (pages 44–45)

Look at the art on page 44. Together, talk about what you are thankful for. Invite your child to draw pictures of or write about these people and things.

Follow the steps above for page 45, inviting your child to show ways of expressing thanks.

We Share God's Word (pages 46–47)

Before reading the Scripture story, explain that Jesus joined other Jewish people for important Jewish feasts. This story takes place during the feast of Passover. Then take turns reading the Scripture story.

Look at the picture and talk about what Jesus is doing. Check your child's understanding of the story by asking: *What do we call the last meal Jesus shared with his disciples? What gift did Jesus give us at the Last Supper?*

STEP 2

We Believe and Celebrate (pages 48–49)

Review what we do in the Introductory Rites and the Liturgy of the Word. Explain that in this chapter your child will be learning about the Liturgy of the Eucharist.

Read aloud the first two paragraphs on page 48. Stress that the Mass is the celebration of the Sacrament of the Eucharist. Call attention to the list of the parts of the Liturgy of the Eucharist.

Explain that, at the beginning of the Liturgy of the Eucharist, the gifts of bread and wine and the altar are prepared. Read aloud the third paragraph on page 48.

Read the first paragraph on page 49. Talk about the prayer and actions of the priest and our response.

Read aloud the last two paragraphs on page 49. Stress that the Mass is a sacrifice and that Jesus' offering of himself on the cross is the greatest sacrifice.

We Believe and Celebrate (pages 50–51)

Read the first paragraph on page 50. Stress that the Eucharistic Prayer is the great prayer of praise and thanksgiving and the Church's most important prayer.

Look at the photos of the priest as you read the text on page 50. Explain that during the consecration the priest says and does what Jesus did at the Last Supper.

Read aloud the first paragraph on page 51. Emphasize that Jesus is really present in the consecrated Bread and Wine. We truly receive Jesus Christ himself in Holy Communion.

Read aloud the remainder of this page. Point out that, when we pray "Amen" at the end of the Eucharistic Prayer, we are saying yes to the prayer the priest has prayed in our name.

Look at the paten and chalice shown. Read the feature *When We Celebrate*. Encourage your child to look at the vessels used by the priest the next time you go to Mass.

STEP 3

We Respond (pages 52–53)

Take turns naming someone or something you will thank God for this Sunday at Mass. Have your child complete the sentence on page 52 by writing or drawing what they will thank God for. Identify these in the space provided.

Identify people and things your family can thank God for. Invite your child to write about or draw them in the space provided on page 53.

We Respond in Prayer (page 54)

Prepare to pray, pausing briefly to think about the time you have spent together.

Pray the Sign of the Cross together. Take the role of Leader and invite your child to pray the responses. Place your hands on your child's head as you pray the prayer of blessing.

Complete the *Sharing Faith with My Family* activities for Chapter 4 on pages 87–88 of the child's text.

CHAPTER 5

Home Lesson Plan

Introduce the Chapter *(page 55)*

Pray together the Sign of the Cross and read the verse from the Mass. Explain that the priest prays these words during the Liturgy of the Eucharist.

Look at the photo of the father and daughter. Suggest that they may be being called into their home to share a family meal. With your child, make up a story about the people in the photo.

STEP 1

We Gather *(pages 56–57)*

Talk about special occasions which were celebrated by enjoying a festive meal together. Read aloud the two sentence starters on page 56. Explain that these sentences may be completed by drawing or writing about one of the family's special events.

Read the sentence starter on page 57. Explain that this sentence may be completed by writing about and/or drawing pictures of what people did at the event. If photos are available, help your child paste them on the page.

We Share God's Word *(pages 58–59)*

Explain that before he returned to his Father in heaven, the risen Jesus visited his disciples several times. Tell your child that the story on page 58 is about one of these visits.

Take turns reading the story. Then look at the illustration. Point out that the risen Jesus, who so amazed the disciples that day, is with us today in the breaking of the Bread at Mass.

STEP 2

We Believe and Celebrate *(pages 60–61)*

Review what happens during the Eucharistic Prayer (See the *We Believe & Celebrate* pages of Chapter 4). Stress that, through the power of the Holy Spirit and the words and actions of the priest, the bread and wine become the Body and Blood of Christ.

Read aloud the first two paragraphs on page 60.

Look at the photo on page 60 which shows people sharing a sign of peace. Then read aloud the third and fourth paragraphs on page 60.

Call attention to the photo of the priest on page 61. Explain that while the priest is breaking the Host, we join with him in praying to Jesus Christ, the Lamb of God. Then read the text on page 61.

We Believe and Celebrate *(pages 62–63)*

Read aloud the first paragraph on page 62. Point out that, through the words "Happy are those who are called to his supper," Jesus invites us to receive his Body and Blood.

Look at the photos on pages 62 and 63. Explain that the children in the photos are showing the proper way to receive Holy Communion. Then read aloud the third and fourth paragraph on page 62 and the first paragraph on page 63. Explain that it is each person's choice to receive from the chalice.

Stress that we should join in the singing of the thanksgiving song. Refer to pages 79 and 80 in the child's text to help demonstrate the proper way to receive Holy Communion.

STEP 3

We Respond *(pages 64–65)*

Talk about all the people in your parish who are helping your child prepare for First Holy Communion. Also discuss ways to thank these helpful people. Then read aloud the two sentence starters on page 64. Help your child complete the sentences by writing and/or drawing.

Ask your child to focus on the day of First Holy Communion. Talk about the people who will be part of the celebration and about what will take place at the church and at home. Help your child complete the sentences on page 65.

We Respond in Prayer *(page 66)*

Prepare to pray. On the prayer table, place a picture or statue of Jesus.

Begin by praying the Sign of the Cross. Then lead the prayer.

Sing or say together the words to "Jesus, You Are Bread for Us," #15 on the *We Believe & Celebrate* CD.

Complete the *Sharing Faith with My Family* activities for Chapter 5 on pages 89–90 of the child's text.

Home Lesson Plan

Introduce the Chapter *(page 67)*

Pray together the Sign of the Cross and the blessing on page 67. Explain that this is part of a blessing that the priest prays over us at the end of every Mass.

Look at the photo of the extended family on page 67. Together write a caption for the photo.

STEP 1

We Gather *(pages 68–69)*

Explain that God has given members of your family special gifts and talents to use to serve others. Talk about the special gifts. Be sure to include skills of cooking or baking, reading and acting out stories, and crafts. Explain that the sentence on page 68 may be completed by writing, drawing pictures and/or pasting photos of family members showing love and care.

Talk about ways friends and neighbors help people. Help your child complete the sentence on page 69 by drawing pictures of, pasting photos of, and/or writing about friends and neighbors serving others.

We Share God's Word *(pages 70–71)*

Look at the illustration on these pages. Explain that the picture shows Jesus with his disciples immediately before his return to his Father in heaven.

Read the story on page 70. Discuss what Jesus wanted his disciples to do.

Stress that Jesus promised his disciples that he would always be with them. Stress that this means us, too. Exclaim how wonderful it is that Jesus is with us always!

STEP 2

We Believe and Celebrate *(pages 72–73)*

Talk about the command Jesus gave to his disciples before his return to his Father in heaven. Then read aloud the first two paragraphs on page 72.

Look at the photo on page 72. Explain that it shows the priest giving the final blessing. Then read the last paragraph on page 72 and the paragraph and the *When We Celebrate* feature on page 73.

Discuss the illustration on page 73. With your child, make up a story about what some of the people may be saying, or describe what your family talks about and does after Mass on Sunday.

We Believe and Celebrate *(pages 74–75)*

Read the paragraphs on page 74. Stress the ways that receiving Jesus in Holy Communion helps us. These ways are described in the second paragraph. Emphasize the importance of receiving Holy Communion as often as possible.

Present the text on page 75. Point out that these are just a few ways in which we can love and serve God and others.

Read the feature, *Most Blessed Sacrament*. The next time you and your child are in church, point out the tabernacle. You will find a prayer to Jesus in the Most Blessed Sacrament on page 96 of the child's text.

STEP 3

We Respond *(pages 76–77)*

Look at a parish bulletin to find ways your parish community joins together to help others. Choose one or two activities in which your family can participate this week. Explain that the sentence on page 76 may be completed by drawing and/or writing about what you will do.

Work together to write a prayer for peace. Help your child copy the words in the space provided at the top of page 77. Then decide on one or two ways your family will share Christ's peace this week. Have your child draw pictures of and/or write about these ways in the appropriate space on page 77.

We Respond in Prayer *(page 78)*

Prepare to pray. Place a plant, a Bible, and a cross on the prayer table.

Pray together the Sign of the Cross. Lead the prayer.

Join in singing or reading aloud the words for "Take the Word of God with You," #16 on the *We Believe & Celebrate* CD. Then share a sign of peace.

Complete the *Sharing Faith with My Family* activities for Chapter 6 on pages 91–92 of the child's text.